JAY HOLMEN

STATEMENT ON ACCOUNTING THEORY AND THEORY ACCEPTANCE

STATEMENT ON ACCOUNTING THEORY AND THEORY ACCEPTANCE

Committee on Concepts and Standards
for External Financial Reports

AMERICAN ACCOUNTING ASSOCIATION

Copyright, American Accounting Association, 1977, All rights reserved
Library of Congress Catalog Card Number 77-747-36
Printed in the United States of America

CONTENTS

PREFACE ix

CHAPTER 1
Introduction 1

CHAPTER 2
Alternative Theory Approaches 5

CHAPTER 3
Criticisms of Present Theory Approaches 31

CHAPTER 4
Difficulties in Achieving Consensus: A General View 41

CHAPTER 5
Implications 49

1976-77
EXECUTIVE COMMITTEE

WILTON T. ANDERSON	CHARLES T. HORNGREN
R. LEE BRUMMET	ALFRED RAPPAPORT
DON T. DeCOSTER	ROSS SKINNER
THOMAS R. DYCKMAN	DAVID SOLOMONS
ROBERT L. GRINAKER	FLOYD W. WINDAL

Preface

This project was initially commissioned by the Executive Committee of the American Accounting Association in 1973. The charge was to write a statement that would provide the same type of survey and distillation of current thinking on accounting theory as *A Statement of Basic Accounting Theory** *(ASOBAT)* provided in an earlier decade. This document represents our response to that assignment.

A periodic reappraisal was deemed necessary since accounting is an important and conceptually rich area and has naturally attracted a wide range of thoughtful and talented researchers. The past ten years have been unusually active in this regard. Fundamental changes have occurred since the publication of ASOBAT. The basic disciplines traditionally utilized by accounting theory have been altered considerably, and accounting researchers have enthusiastically employed their new tools, perspectives, and analytical techniques to explore a wide range of accounting issues from new directions.

In our view, these changes are exciting and indicative of intellectual growth. Yet, they are also frustrating since the new knowledge gathered during the past decade amply testifies to the view that there are no easy theoretical answers to many of the urgent problems faced by the profession.

For this reason, ours is not a statement *of* accounting theory; instead we have prepared a statement *about* accounting theory and theory acceptance. This distinction is a natural consequence of the recent advances in knowledge. Just as a synthesis of leading thought ten years ago led to an ASOBAT-type document, an equally conscientious synthesis of today's research findings generates this current statement. While different in terms of scope, mode of analysis, and conclusions, this document—like ASOBAT—is intended to be a faithful rendition of the frontiers of accounting theory at the time it is written.

The committee has worked on this document for two years. We have met as an entire group eight times and have had several subcommittee meetings. Numerous drafts have been written and rewritten, edited, and re-edited. It is our hope that the final product not only synthesizes the predominant theory perspectives in the contemporary literature but also serves as an educational document for students of accounting thought.

This report benefited from the editorial suggestions of Lanny G. Chasteen and Jean Eros. Much of the groundwork for this document was developed by a predecessor committee in 1973-74 under the chairmanship of Kermit Larson. In addition to most of the members of the current group, that committee also included Enrico Petri, Gary L. Sundem and Jan R. Williams. Their contributions, as well as the excellent guidance provided by Kermit Larson, are gratefully acknowledged.

Lawrence Revsine, Chairman
Committee on Concepts and
Standards for External Financial Reports

---

* Committee to Prepare A Statement of Basic Accounting Theory, *A Statement of Basic Accounting Theory* (American Accounting Association, 1966).

**Committee on Concepts and Standards for
External Financial Reports**

Statement on Accounting Theory and Theory Acceptance

Members:		
	James R. Boatsman	Oklahoma State University
	Joel Demski	Stanford University
	John W. Kennelly	DePaul University
	Kermit D. Larson	University of Texas, Austin
	Lawrence Revsine, Chairman	Northwestern University
	George J. Staubus	University of California, Berkeley
	Robert R. Sterling	Rice University
	Jerry J. Weygandt	University of Wisconsin, Madison
	Stephen A. Zeff	Tulane University

The views expressed in this report are those of a majority of the committee members. Publication in this volume does not imply agreement or official endorsement on the part of the American Accounting Association or its Executive Committee.

Chapter 1

Introduction

There has been a persistent, widely held belief among accountants that the accumulation of accounting theory literature would eventually lead to a compelling basis for specifying the content of external financial reports. Indeed, a primary objective implicit in the charge to this committee was to ascertain the extent to which existing accounting theories do in fact provide a basis for determining the content of external financial reports and resolving accounting controversies.

If a compelling conceptual basis could be discerned, the committee would then identify the basic concepts that should underlie the design of external reports. Alternatively, if the theoretical literature of accounting has not provided a sufficient basis for guiding the design of external reports, the committee would then assess the plausible reasons for this state of affairs.

In the view of this committee, a single universally accepted basic accounting theory does not exist at this time. Instead, a multiplicity of theories has been—and continues to be—proposed. Therefore, this statement cannot provide accounting with an unequivocally acceptable conceptual superstructure when the underlying foundation has not yet settled. Accordingly, we have defined our task to be somewhat different from past theory statements. Herein we seek to explain why the accounting community has been unable to achieve theoretical closure. That is, we attempt to explore the problem that characterizes theoretical debate at this stage of accounting development: virtually endless argumentation and inability to resolve issues that are raised. Once the nature of the problem is better and more widely understood, we believe that unrealistic expectations regarding "authoritative *theory* pronouncements" will be reduced. While we most emphatically do *not* call for a moratorium on theory building and conceptual modeling, we do call for a better understanding of the reasons why such efforts in the past seem to have persuaded only a small proportion of the intended audience.

We believe that theory *acceptance* would not be facilitated by this committee's attempting to impose theory closure. Numerous theories already exist. Selection of one such theory by this committee might be persuasive to some. However, because of the complex nature of the process of theory acceptance (which is discussed in Chapter 4), any imposed selection of one from among competing theories would not resolve existing debates and would not provide rigorously defensible theoretical closure. Accordingly, this report does not attempt to develop a statement *of* universally accepted accounting theory; instead ours is a statement *about* accounting theory and theory acceptance. Specifically, we explore certain theoretical approaches to accounting and explain the reasons why achieving consensus is an arduous task.

Basis for Different Accounting Theories

There is currently an abundance of theories of external reporting. At a very general level, accounting writers appear to agree that the central purpose of financial accounting is the systematic provision of economic data about reporting entities. The data are provided to individuals and groups external to the reporting entity, and it is generally acknowledged that profit-seeking as well as not-for-profit entities may be involved.

However, when one attempts to apply this doctrine to resolve actual accounting issues, divergent theories arise. Such divergence results from differences in the way people specify both the "users" of accounting data and the "environment" in which preparers and users of accounting data are thought to behave.

In this section we survey alternative characterizations of "user" and "environment." The differences in specifications that we observe among writers and the variety of analyses induced by these divergences lead us to conclude that:

1. no single governing theory of finan-

cial accounting is rich enough to encompass the full range of user-environment specifications effectively; hence,

2. there exists in the financial accounting literature not *a theory* of financial accounting, but *a collection of theories* which can be arrayed over the differences in user-environment specifications.

Users

The set of users of financial accounting reports sometimes is defined narrowly to include only the present owners of a reporting entity; at other times, it is defined broadly to include creditors, employees, regulatory and taxing authorities, charitable institutions, and the "general public."

Further, there is some question about what constitutes "use" of accounting data. It is apparent that individuals who do not actually receive the accounting data in question can be affected by the actions of those who do receive and act upon those data. (Insider trading is a classic example of this phenomenon.) The notion of "use" of accounting data can be broadened, therefore, to encompass those affected indirectly by the appearance and employment of the data by those having direct access. In the limit, then, the entire membership of a society may be regarded as constituting the universal set of "users"; future generations might well be included.[1]

With homogeneous users, or heterogeneous users who happen to agree on the financial data they want, the resolution of accounting issues is fairly straightforward. The preferences of a "representative" individual will govern, because all individuals are—by assumption—unanimous in their preferences for financial reporting. But with heterogeneity, the problem becomes quite complex.

Even when the population of users is specified, a number of questions about the behavior of users remain. For example, to what extent do beliefs and preferences vary across users and how, if at all, do differences in users' beliefs and preferences affect the demand for and use of accounting reports? When faced with an accounting report, how do users react? Are they influenced by the "form" as well as "content" of the data presented? Are they "rational" processors of the data? Do they adopt "naive" interpretive processes or "sophisticated" processes? When faced with multiple sources of data, how do they combine the various data into a composite assessment? Furthermore, do answers to these questions change when we look at users in the aggregate rather than individually?

To illustrate the importance of these issues to theory construction, consider the following. While questions about where certain data should be disclosed within a report may be crucial if one view of user behavior is assumed, they may be irrelevant if another view were adopted. For example, a rational processor, uninfluenced by form, would be totally indifferent to the disclosure of data in footnotes rather than in the statement proper. Similarly, questions of whether financial reports should just portray events, or portray and interpret events, become interesting or uninteresting depending on one's view of user behavior.

In a "general" theory, the specification of users should be able to cope with a va-

---

[1] However, this observation does not imply that focusing upon a subset, even a quite narrow subset, of this broad group is undesirable *per se*. On the contrary, given the purpose of the analysis and the audience to which it is addressed, such a restriction may be either theoretically sound or pragmatically dictated.

We can say that the focus (on a subject) is "theoretically sound" if it can be shown to be based upon: first a decomposition of the set of all users into subsets; and second, an analytical separation of the subset to be considered from the other subsets. For example, can we focus upon "naive" users without also giving direct attention to the impact(s) that they have upon "sophisticated" users, and/or those impacts which the actions of sophisticated users have upon them? The possibility of *interactive* effect can seriously weaken, if not destroy, the efficacy of focusing on a subset.

Even where theoretical soundness would be weakened by focusing on a subset, the focus may be "pragmatically justified" where the losses in "theoretical soundness" are more than offset by the gains in tractability in the analysis (in the judgment of those formulating and those intending to employ the theory).

Introduction

riety of individual and multi-person configurations. Such a strong requirement implies that if a "general" theory is to exist and survive it should accommodate what is known or believed about the *variety* of users. Indeed, such a theory should be able to cope with and say something about the desirability of a variety of institutional arrangements as well. Several critical questions are empirical and largely unexplored. As a consequence, several accounting theories—each incorporating highly specific views of user behavior—coexist. And the views of user behavior are usually inconsistent across the theories that employ this approach.

Environment

A similar set of observations may be made when we examine the environment in which users and preparers of accounting data are thought to behave.

One prominent environmental issue concerns the existence of competing sources of information about the entity in question. Some theories do not explicitly consider alternative sources of financial information; others actively examine accounting information as one of several sources of financial information. Similarly, in examining accounting information, some theories focus on the preparers of such information while others treat them passively.

In a multiple-source setting, considerations of efficiency would imply that accounting systems should be oriented to reporting those attributes of the entity for which they have a comparative advantage over other sources, either as a primary source of "news" or as an instrument for confirming (or disconfirming) "news" reported by more timely sources.

Another environmental issue concerns the nature of the multi-person setting for actions by users. Both "market" interactions (exchanges) and "nonmarket" interactions (externalities) appear to be present in relationships among preparers and users. With respect to market interactions, such questions as the following are asked: To what extent are securities markets "efficient" in reflecting available information? What is the nature of the market for information? In particular, do we observe market failure to such a degree that intervention is socially desirable?[2]

With respect to "externalities," to what extent are nonmarket interactions among users present? To what extent are they pertinent? Externalities may also exist among preparers. Information conveyed by one source may affect that from another. Similarly, reporting for income tax purposes, for example, can interact with financial reporting. Also, there is an interaction between managers' decisions and external financial reports.

A third class of issues deals with attributes of accounting processes, and of the control of such processes. We should recognize, for example, that auditing is an accepted component of the external reporting environment and, by implication, that reporting concerns cannot be separated from auditing concerns. We must also seek to understand the many environment-user influences that have an impact upon auditing if we are subsequently to understand the nature of auditing's influence on reporting.

Summary

It is easy to obtain agreement on the broad role of financial accounting, as well as on the fact that accounting systems are "costly," and hence that their design presents a class of resource allocation problems. Such agreement, however, overlooks the existence of basic differences in the way various theories view users and the preparer-user environments. One's specifications of users and environment are integral to the modeling of accounting choices and will significantly shape the resulting theories.

What we seek is a theory that is general enough to cope with this variety and specific enough to offer assistance to accounting policy makers. But none of the available theories is acceptable to all accountants.

---

[2] A market failure is said to exist when the market-determined production and consumption levels generate an inefficient allocation of resources. See Beaver and Demski (1974) and Gonedes, Dopuch, and Penman (1975) for further discussion of market failure considerations.

Instead, we have a collection of theories, each perhaps capable of coping with aspects of this specification problem, but only by sacrificing attention to others.

Chapter 2

Alternative Theory Approaches

In this chapter we classify accounting theories and summarize the dominant approaches that have evolved within each of the classifications. We have discerned three basic theoretical approaches: (1) classical ("true income" and inductive) models; (2) decision usefulness; and (3) information economics.[1] This survey is intended to provide the foundation necessary for our subsequent examination of the reasons that the profession has been unable to achieve consensus on a "general" theory of external reporting.

Classical Approaches to Theory Development

"The history [of accounting thought]," writes Chambers, "is not a history of development, but a series of disconnected episodes" (1965, p. 33). The authors of early accounting theories failed to supply a developmental thread from one argument to the next. Few referred to the works of others, and none built explicitly on the writings of predecessors or contemporaries in the accounting literature.

At the outset, it will be useful to classify a number of major writers discussed in this section according to their roles within the literature. We begin by chronologically listing their principal writings:

William A. Paton, *Accounting Theory — With Special Reference to the Corporate Enterprise* (1922).
Henry Rand Hatfield, *Accounting — Its Principles and Problems* (1927).
John B. Canning, *The Economics of Accountancy* (1929).

Henry W. Sweeney, *Stabilized Accounting* (1936).
Stephen Gilman, *Accounting Concepts of Profit* (1939).
Kenneth MacNeal, *Truth in Accounting* (1939).
W. A. Paton and A. C. Littleton, *An Introduction to Corporate Accounting Standards* (1940).
Sidney S. Alexander, "Income Measurement in A Dynamic Economy" (1950).
A. C. Littleton, *Structure of Accounting Theory* (1953).
Edgar O. Edwards and Philip W. Bell, *The Theory and Measurement of Business Income* (1961).
Maurice Moonitz, *The Basic Postulates of Accounting* (1961).
Robert T. Sprouse and Maurice Moonitz, *A Tentative Set of Broad Accounting Principles for Business Enterprises* (1962).
Yuji Ijiri, *Theory of Accounting Measurement* (1975).

Writers such as Paton, Sweeney, MacNeal, Edwards and Bell, Moonitz, and Sprouse are advocates: they have argued for the primacy of new theories or approaches. They have been, in every sense, reformers. Canning and Alexander, by contrast, are more analysts and explicators than advocates. They analyze and assess what accountants do and seek to do, they undertake to explain an economic model to accountants, and they conclude by endeavoring to adapt the economic model to the pragmatic world of the accountant. All the writers in this first group are normative theorists. They are primarily deductivists. Canning and Alexander differ from the rest of the group more in degree than in kind; they are motivated less by missionary zeal than by a desire to analyze, criticize, and suggest.

Hatfield, Gilman, Littleton, the Paton-Littleton partnership, and Ijiri are chiefly positivist, inductive writers, some of whom

---

[1] We should observe that some authors who have helped develop these approaches may disavow any intention of having contributed to an accounting theory. Nevertheless, each of these approaches has variously been perceived as a potential source of a theory of accounting or as a basis for determining the content of external financial reporting. The widespread acceptance of these perceptions leads the committee, tentatively at least, to recognize each as an approach to theorizing in accounting.

interpose occasional normative deductive reasoning derived from unstated premises. Of the five, Gilman and Hatfield induce at a more concrete level of generalization than the other three; they summarize, compare, and expose elements of illogic and inconsistency; they seek to rationalize diverse theories and practices. Littleton, Paton-Littleton, and Ijiri, contrariwise, undertake to develop coherent theories of extant practice.

What problems do these authors explore? To the inductivists, when they do not interpose normative deductive reasoning, the problems are *perforce* those that are implicitly being addressed in actual accounting practice. In the process of induction, however, the authors may disagree over generalized principles and goals. To the normative deductivists, the answer is less evident. In the broadest terms, both deductivists and inductivists are concerned with designing financial reports that communicate pertinent information to a set of readers.

Why did many of the prominent theorists advocate current costs or values? To a significant degree, they may have been influenced by the neoclassical economic theory of the firm, in which historical costs are ignored entirely. They may have observed the behavior of investors and other economic decision makers and concluded with a validated hypothesis that such decision makers seek current value, not historical cost, information. No findings from any formal hypothesis testing are reported; prior to the 1960s, it was not customary for accounting writers to conduct such research. Unlike the later group of normative writers who embraced a decision-usefulness approach, the early normative writers did not inquire deeply into the decisional framework of users. They posited the existence of specified users, and proceeded to argue that current values are a superior type of information to historical costs. As we will note below, pragmatic considerations obliged several of the writers to soften their recommendations.

Normative Deductive School

In the first decades of the century, most accounting writers dealt with the particulars of accounting practice rather than with conceptual underpinnings. Accounting theory, especially in the majority of textbooks, consisted of special pleadings, without an evident trail of logic, for or against specific accounting practices. Doctrine was defended against heretics.

The development of a coherent accounting theory may have been thought by practitioners to be a task more suited to the academic mind. In fact, academic accountants prior to the 1950s were a dichotomous lot. Most accounting professors in American universities were far more oriented towards practice than towards academic research. Many were former practitioners or were contemporaneously engaged in accounting practice. A comparatively small number of academics possessed doctorates.

Only a relatively few universities awarded doctorates in business administration or commerce before the 1950s — and most of those appear to have required a strong dose of economic theory. Thus, many of the early doctorates awarded to accounting academics, to Hatfield and Paton, for example, were in economics. It should come as no surprise, therefore, that economic theory would influence to a considerable degree the deductive writings of those comparatively few academics who challenged doctrine with coherent accounting theories. Indeed, several of the most prominent writers, notably Canning and Alexander, were economists.

The deductive theorists, with the exception of Alexander (see Appendix), concluded that income measured using a single valuation base would ideally meet the needs of all users. In that regard, they have sometimes been described as advocates of a "true income" theory. (A summary analysis of their respective positions is given in Exhibit I.) They drew on the teachings of neoclassical economic theory and on their observations of economic behavior to propose that accounting, which had been preoccupied with historical record-keeping and conservative reckonings, should be reconstructed to reflect current costs or values. They borrowed from economics the terms "income" and

EXHIBIT I
Summary Analysis of the Approaches of the Deductive Theorists

Name	Inferred User(s)	Inferred Model under Ideal Circumstances	Recommended Measurement Methods
Paton (1922)	To promote efficient management, which furthers the interests of all equity holders; also as a report on enterprise progress to equity holders.	"Income in the broadest sense may be conceived as including the entire net increase in the [true economic position of a business] after due allowance has been made for new investments and withdrawals" (pp. 440, 464).	Include appreciation of marketable securities and standard raw materials in non-operating income; to recognize appreciation on other inventories would be more dubious; appreciation on fixed assets and the consequent depreciation on appreciation might be displayed in a supplementary statement.
Canning (1929)	"The proprietor and those beneficially interested in proprietorship wish chiefly to know what *net changes in power to command future final income have occurred within a year by reason of the enterprise activities*" (pp. 169-170).	Measure the annual change in capital value by reference to the direct valuation of the assets.	Measure assets and liabilities by discounting future cash flows, if feasible; if not, resort to indirect valuations (such as cost). Income is the change in net assets.
Sweeney (1936)	All users, but primarily business management.	Measure changes in the real valuation of capital by reference to changes in its future productivity to the marginal user.	Account for changes in replacement cost (which are denominated as unrealized until the assets are exchanged); also use GPL changes.
MacNeal (1939)	"To inform the owners of a business of all the profits and losses in which they have an equity" (p. 299); other parties (esp. managers and creditors) at interest also have a right to the same information (pp. 180-182).	Measure changes in "economic value," defined as the market prices of the firm's assets in a free, competitive, broad, and active market.	Use market price for "marketable assets," appraisals or replacement cost for "reproducible, non-marketable assets," and original cost less amortization or depletion for "non-reproducible, non-marketable assets." Would include unrealized holding gains and losses on merchandise inventory in net income; other unrealized items, while disclosed in the income statement, are transferred to Capital Surplus.
Alexander (1950)	Asserts different incomes for different purposes where economy is characterized by changing prices and changing expectations of future earning power.	Measure the capitalized value of the enterprise and changes therein.	Proposes various measures depending on user and use. Is skeptical of the usefulness of GPL accounting.
Edwards/Bell (1961)	To facilitate management planning and to assist security analysts, owners of business firms, and potential entrepreneurs in making rational comparisons among companies and industries.	Measure the subjective value and subjective profit of the enterprise.	Account for changes in replacement cost, distinguishing between (1) the excess of realized revenue over the current replacement cost of non-monetary assets consumed, and (2) the unrealized changes in the replacement cost of non-monetary assets. The grand total is called "business profit." Also use GPL changes.
Moonitz (1961) Sprouse/ Moonitz (1962)	To facilitate management planning and control, and to aid owners, creditors, and government in evaluating management performance.	Measure the changes in enterprise wealth, evidently being the present value of future cash flows.	Use discounted present value (at historical interest rates) for receivables and payables to be settled in cash, net realizable values for readily salable inventories, and replacement cost for other inventories and for tangible fixed assets. Reject realization as lacking "analytical precision." Also favor GPL changes.

"wealth" and sought to make them operational in an accounting context. In the act of rendering them operational, they disagreed on particulars. Their differences over how to reduce abstract concepts to pragmatic recommendations perhaps reflected their conclusions about users' economic behavior. Doubtless they had different perceptions of the accessibility of acceptable data. Paton, MacNeal, and Sprouse and Moonitz appealed to the market as the pertinent source of information.

Canning, Sweeney, Alexander, Edwards and Bell, and Moonitz were more influenced by the vision of capital as the present value of future incomes. In theory, however, asset prices correspond with capitalized future incomes only under very restrictive conditions. Thus, the differences in the specific policy recommendations of Paton, Canning, Sweeney, MacNeal, Alexander, Edwards and Bell, Moonitz, and Sprouse and Moonitz can be traced to the relaxations in conceptual rigor which they believe to be warranted by the presence of uncertainty.

Several of the writers cite particular users (ordinarily shareholders, creditors, and managers) and occasionally suggest the information that users would find useful; however, it is not possible to employ these casual references to explain the surrogate choices that the writers made. Typically, the pragmatic modifications in a model are matter-of-factly asserted by the writer. Except in the case of Alexander, who proposes different models for different users, each writer offers his policy recommendation as a universally valid proposal, as if the entire hierarchy of users would be sufficiently well served by the resulting information. Nothing was said about the possible repercussions on resource allocation decisions made elsewhere in society as a consequence of decisions taken on the basis of information generated by a model.

What factors did the writers regard as influential in shaping their policy recommendations? Paton — and perhaps Sweeney — opted for replacement cost in preference to net realizable value in order not to recognize gross margin prior to realization. In that respect, Paton and Sweeney are more conservative than is generally believed. Both attached considerable importance to the distinction between realized and unrealized outcomes. Sweeney was under pressure from his dissertation adviser to be "practical," and his book *Stabilized Accounting* was a product of the dissertation (see Appendix).

Canning had a dual mission: to lend advice to the profession as an economist, and to interpret accountants' handiwork to other economists. He acknowledged that it would seldom be possible for accountants to compute the capitalized values of nonmonetary assets. He therefore proposed a method of indirect valuation by which an asset would be assessed at the current cost to reacquire by the least costly means the remaining services inherent in the asset. This approach, Canning believed, constituted a sound application of the economist's opportunity cost analysis, and he devoted the latter part of his book to the practical problems of implementation.

Edwards and Bell imposed upon themselves the constraint that the accounting profession not be revulsed by their policy recommendation; consequently, like Paton and Sweeney, they proposed a replacement cost system in which gross margin would not be recognized until sale. But unlike Paton and Sweeney, they preferred to include in income the currently accrued holding gain on nonmonetary assets.

MacNeal had been a practicing accountant; he alone among the deductive writers did not possess a doctorate. To MacNeal, "truth" was ascertainable in current markets; he shared the practitioner's aversion to relying on management's opinion of the values of assets. He recommended replacement costs — and, as a last resort, historical costs — only when acceptable market selling prices were not accessible (see Appendix).

An interesting comparison may be drawn among the deductive writers according to whether their orientation was toward income-statement analysis or comparative balance-sheet analysis. Paton and Sweeney, oriented toward income statements, were mindful of the accountant's reluctance to record or report unrealized gross margins and unrealized holding gains. MacNeal, Edwards and Bell, Moonitz, and Sprouse and Moonitz were inclined to view accounting as a succession of balance sheets. It is therefore not surprising that they would include unrealized holding gains in net income and, except for Edwards and Bell's preoccupation with the reaction of the accounting profession to their proposed system, they would have been unanimous in their disavowal of the conventional realization concept.

Of the deductive theorists, only Alexander proposed that different models might be needed for different users. Yet he only intimates how and why different users might require different information; he stops well short of constructing decision models.

It may be observed that the deductive writers operated independently of one another, rarely comparing their work with that of predecessors or contemporaries. The logic of their analyses is difficult to monitor, as it reflects implicit criteria and judgments. Of their writings, it may be said that they neither proved their points nor were disproven by others. A common thread may be discerned in their diverse recommendations: the implicit agreement that users seek (or should seek) current-price information in making economic decisions. In this important respect, notwithstanding the diversity of their recommendations, their cause was united.

Inductive School

Hatfield and Gilman are inductivists in a special sense. They were annotators of the literature. They compared and contrasted different practices and policy recommendations, drew attention to similar and discordant notes among diverse sources of authority, and commented upon illogic and inconsistencies in practice and in the literature. While they did not attempt to formulate coherent theories of extant practice, they did endeavor to identify gaps and (Hatfield especially) to distinguish doctrine from principle.

Littleton, upon observing the evolution of accounting practice over a considerable period of time, concluded that the accountant endeavors to help the readers of financial reports understand the business enterprise by confining his measures to objectively verifiable transactions to which the firm is a party. By a largely implicit argument of a normative variety, Littleton maintained that accounting reports can best serve the needs of those who contemplate future actions by reporting factually on the immediate consequences of actions previously taken by the firm. Current prices and index numbers are either irrelevant to the transactional experience of the enterprise or are not susceptible to objective measurement; their inclusion in financial statements would disturb the homogeneity of the contents and might well reduce the integrity of the objectively determined historical results.

Littleton induced accounting principles from observing accounting practice, and argued in a normative deductive vein that the goals implicit in this generalized practice should be retained. He seemed to be concerned that an accounting that deals with actual transactions could become debauched by integrating in the financial reports subjective judgments about the impact of economic forces on the enterprise. While Littleton is remembered primarily as a historian and an inductive theorist, his persistent defense of the generalized principles induced from actual practice partake of normative deductive logic developed from unstated premises. In that respect, he has been characterized as proposing an "accounting Darwinism." According to this view, accounting is continually in evolution, and the elements that have withstood the succession of challengers have, at least thus far, earned a place in current practice.

When a predominantly deductive writer of decidedly strong views (Paton) and a predominantly inductive writer possessing equally strong views (Littleton) join in the writing of a monograph, a compromise methodology should not be unexpected. The resulting monograph (1940), probably the most influential work in American accounting literature, was a rationalization of then extant accounting practice, explicated at a level of theoretical abstraction that had known few precedents. The elegance of the writers' generalizations even deceived a leading practicing accountant who, in a review of the monograph for a journal, asserted that it bore no perceptible relation to current practice. Indeed, the work never could have attained the degree of popularity it has since enjoyed had it not been a largely faithful induction of actual accounting practice, even despite an occasional oughtness spliced into the exposition. In addition, vivid metaphors employed in the inductive exercise (e.g., "matching," "attaching," "costs are assembled... as if they had a power of cohesion") conferred a greater respectability on practices that could be so colorfully and attractively characterized. (A more detailed analysis of this monograph is given in the Appendix to this chapter.)

In comparison with Littleton, Ijiri (1975) shows a clearer separation of deductive and inductive reasoning. Ijiri undertakes to generalize the goals implicit in current accounting practice, and then defends historical cost against the criticisms of current-cost and current value advocates by a reverse-inductive analysis. The defense is embedded in the particular manner of his induction. Ijiri concludes that accounting practice may best be interpreted in terms of accountability, which he defines as economic performance measurement that is not susceptible to manipulation by interested parties. Unequivocal and unambiguous measures are viewed as the *sine qua non* of accountability. The continuous recording of current values is rejected because they are predicated on hypothetical actions of the entity and, as such, are not verifiable. Ijiri explains forthrightly his strategy for preferring inductive to deductive reasoning:

> This type of inductive reasoning to derive goals implicit in the behavior of an existing system is not intended to be pro-establishment or to promote the maintenance of the status quo. The purpose of such an exercise is to highlight where changes are most needed and where they are feasible. Changes suggested as a result of such a study have a much better chance of being actually implemented. Goal assumptions in normative models or goals advocated in policy discussions are often stated purely on the basis of one's conviction and preference, rather than on the basis of inductive study of the existing system. This may perhaps be the most crucial reason why so many normative models or policy proposals are not implemented in the real world. (p. 28)

Other Possible Approaches

It is sometimes suggested that "postulates and principles" should be viewed as a fundamentally distinct approach to theory development. Yet it may represent nothing more than a different packaging of the deductive methodology and could accommodate either the "true income" or "decision model" approach. "Postulates and principles" could also be adopted as the framework for developing a hierarchy of generalizations in an inductive study.

Summary

Two approaches to theory development may be discerned apart from the more recent emergence of decision-usefulness formulations, which are discussed in the following sections of this chapter. These are the "true income" (an example of the normative deductive school) and the inductive methodologies. The former attempts to formulate implicit accounting models of global application, while the latter attempts to rationalize, and sometimes even to justify (by the interposition of normative deductive reasoning), major elements of extant accounting practice.

The Decision-Usefulness Approach

Another approach by which accounting theory has been generated is based on explicit recognition of the usefulness objective. The decision-usefulness approach is a broad one from which two major branches arise. In the first, decision *models* are stressed. Information relevant to a decision model or criterion is isolated and various accounting alternatives are compared to the data presumably necessary for implementing these decision models. In the second branch of the decision-usefulness approach, decision *makers* are the focus of attention. Their reactions to alternative accounting data are studied as a means for inductively deriving preferred reporting alternatives.

Decision Models

Most of the earliest research on decision-usefulness implicitly adopted the decision *model* emphasis although the assumed decision model was often not specified in detail. This approach first began to appear in the literature in the 1950s. By 1973 it had achieved both professional recognition and broad exposure through publication of the report of the American Institute of Certified Public Accountants (AICPA) Study Group on the Objectives of Financial Statements (1973). In that document, also known as the Trueblood Report, it was stated that "the basic objective of financial statements is to provide information useful for making economic decisions" (p. 13).

Prior to the 1950s, a number of carefully prepared works on accounting theory did refer to users of accounting outputs, but the theoretical structures in those works were not demonstrably based on the alleged information "needs" of users. Several instances of passing references to users and the uses of financial information will serve to illustrate that practice. The 1936 "Tentative Statement" of the American Accounting Association (AAA) included, but did not build upon, this paragraph:

> The most important applications of accounting principles lie in the field of corporate accounting, particularly in the preparation of published reports of profits and financial position. On the interpretation of such reports depend so many vital decisions of business and government that they have come to be of great economic and social significance. (p. 187)

The 1941 AAA statement reiterated this point, again without subsequent development (p. 133).

The Sanders, Hatfield, and Moore monograph (1938) was more explicit in recognizing the groups who have information "needs" in relation to an entity. The authors' list of functions of accounting included:

> ... preparing from time to time statements showing all the more important aspects of the capital and income of the business and of the legal equities in them, satisfying thereby the need for information of all the parties in interest, especially of:
>
> (a) the management of the business,
> (b) outside groups, such as investors and creditors,
> (c) government, in such matters as taxation and regulation. (p. 4)

Paton and Littleton (1940) gave user needs even more prominent attention, including them in their statement of the purpose of accounting:

> The purpose of accounting is to furnish financial data concerning a business enterprise, compiled and presented to meet the needs of management, investors, and the public. (p. 1)

May (1943, pp. 19-21) went still further when he listed ten "uses of financial accounts," such as "to determine the legality of dividends" and "as a basis for price or rate regulation." May followed that enumeration with a chapter on "The Uses of Accounts and Their Influence on Accounting," although he did not model decision processes or use decision models and their information requirements as a basis for accounting theory.

Vatter (1947, pp. 7-9) also gave a good deal of attention to the uses of accounting — in management, in the various taxing and social control activities of governments, and in the general area of credit extension and investment — but he rejected the idea of basing a general theory on any particular point of view. Instead, he developed the operations-oriented "fund theory," which ignores all user groups in an effort to be impersonal and unbiased. This theory later provided part of the basis for the "data bank" and "events theory" approaches to accounting.

During the 1950s there was a strong user-oriented movement in the managerial accounting literature. That movement may have served as the stimulus for the initial acceptance of the decision-usefulness objective in external reporting at that time. Early works include a doctoral dissertation (Staubus, 1954) and Chambers' article, "Blueprint for a Theory of Accounting," published in 1955, which stressed that "the basic function of accounting ... [is] the provision of information to be used in making rational decisions" (p. 25). The July 1955 issue of *The Accounting Review* included the Committee on Concepts and Standards' Supplementary Statement No. 8:

Since the ultimate test of the quality of any communication is its effectiveness in conveying pertinent information, the initial step in the development of standards of disclosure for published financial statements is the establishment of the purposes to be served. The potential users of corporate reports include governmental agencies, short- and long-term creditors, labor organizations, stockholders, and potential investors. Since in all likelihood the needs of these groups cannot be served equally well by a single set of statements, the interest of some one audience should be identified as primary. Traditionally, this has been the stockholder group....

In considering disclosure standards, therefore, the Committee has been concerned primarily with the use of financial statements (1) in making investment decisions and (2) in the exercise of investor control over management. (p. 401)

The Committee's acceptance of the user orientation was not merely superficial; it shaped the entire Statement. However, the next major statement of the Committee on Concepts and Standards, issued in 1957, ignored the user approach except in the last section, "Standards of Disclosure," which was based on Supplementary Statement No. 8. As a result, AAA literature did not contribute heavily to the acceptance of the decision-usefulness approach to accounting theory until *A Statement of Basic Accounting Theory* was published in 1966. Chambers' "Blueprint" article might well have served as the starting point for a decision-usefulness theory of financial accounting:

> ... a formal information-providing system should conform with two general propositions.
>
> The first is a condition of all logical discourse. The system should be logically consistent; no rule or process can be permitted which is contrary to any other rule or process....
>
> The second proposition arises from the use of accounting statements as a basis for making decisions of practical consequence. The information yielded by any such system should be relevant to the kinds of decision the making of which it is expected to facilitate. (pp. 21-22)

When considering "the introduction of additional rules, . . . in every case the test is required to be: 'What is necessary for rational decision-making' " (p. 24). While that view provided an excellent foundation for the development of a detailed decision model approach, in his subsequent works Chambers apparently rejected the idea of basing an accounting theory on the decision models of specific user groups. Instead, he emphasized the general usefulness of "current cash equivalents" much in the manner in which MacNeal accepted current market values and Canning accepted the present value measure of capital. Chambers explained that "the effect of the arguments of this book is to shift the focus of attention from the parties of interest (creditors, investors, managers) to the entity under consideration . . ." (1966, p. 375). "To provide the corroborable and corroborated financial statements which will serve as foundations for everyman's evaluations and actions is the business of the kind of accounting here envisaged" (1966, p. 376).

Work on the decision-usefulness approach eventually led to more specific reliance on decision models. Staubus (1961) emphasized that "accountants should explicitly and continuously recognize an objective or objectives of accounting," and "that a major objective of accounting is to provide quantitative economic information that will be useful in making investment decisions" (p. viii). He then constructed an interrelated set of basic concepts and described a cash-flow-oriented measurement system keyed to the dominant theme of finance theory of the time — the discounting view of securities value. This led to the position that the attribute of assets and liabilities that is most relevant to security investment decisions is discounted future cash flows.

The current status of the decision-usefulness, decision model approach to accounting theory may be summarized as follows:

1. The primary objective of accounting is to provide financial information about the economic affairs of an entity to interested parties for use in making decisions. This objective statement is a premise which most people seem to find acceptable, subject to slight variations. But it may not be suitable unless one interprets "decisions" broadly. For "decisions" to encompass what might be called the control objective, the term must include making choices regarding the investigation of variances, choices by employees of the honest or dishonest course, and choices as to treatment of offending employees. If such an interpretation is not acceptable, a second objective — the control objective — must be given equal billing.

2. To be useful in making decisions, financial information must possess several normative qualities. The primary one is the relevance to the particular decision at hand of the attribute selected for measurement. The secondary one is the reliability of the measurement of the (relevant) attribute. Objectivity, verifiability, freedom from bias, and accuracy are terms for overlapping parts of the reliability quality. Other qualities, such as comparability, understandability, timeliness, and economy, are also emphasized. A set of such desirable qualities is used as criteria for evaluating alternative accounting methods.

3. The relevance criterion is used to select the attribute(s) of an object or event to be emphasized in financial reporting. Information about an attribute of an object or event is relevant to a decision if knowledge of that attribute can help the decision maker determine alternative courses of action or to evaluate an outcome of an alternative course of action. Selection of the attribute most relevant to a decision requires familiarity with the decision processes of the user of financial data. "Modeling" decision processes is often helpful to accounting theorists.

4. The decision-usefulness approach provides for the development of theory on the basis of knowledge of decision processes of investors, taxing authorities, union negotiators, regulatory agencies, and other external users of accounting data, as well as managers. To date, however, only the decisions of investors (in the broad sense) have served as the basis for fairly complete theories of external reporting.

5. The investment decision models utilized by decision-usefulness theorists have been either simple present value models or two-parameter expected return and risk models. Risk has not been formally incorporated in accounting theories to any great extent; expected future cash flows to investors have. Building on these common decision-usefulness aspects, various writers have followed alternative paths.

6. Investors' desires to predict cash flows from the firm have led many decision-usefulness theorists to a cash flow orientation (Staubus, 1961; AAA, 1969; Revsine, 1973; Study Group on the Objectives of Financial Statements, 1973).

Cash returns to investors depend upon the firm's capacity to pay, which, in turn, depends upon its present cash balance and its cash flow potentials. Present cash and positive cash flow potentials are assets; negative cash flow potentials are liabilities. When reliable evidence of future cash flows is available it should be used in the measurement of an asset or a liability. Otherwise, a surrogate measurement method must be used. Accordingly, several studies have explored the theoretical conditions under which various financial measurement alternatives would tend to provide surrogates for future cash flows (Revsine, 1970a, 1973; Staubus, 1967, 1971).

When the measurements of all assets and liabilities reflect or have some relation to cash flow potential, the difference—owners' equity—has some relation to the cash flow potential of the owners' interests. Revenues, expenses, and income, as changes in net assets, are estimates of the change in the net cash flow potential of the firm from operating activities.

7. One variant of the cash flow approach (Revsine, 1973) concentrates on "distributable operating flows" as a major basis for dividends. Distributable operating flows make up "that portion of net operating flows which can be distributed to owners without reducing future physical operating levels" (p. 47).

Maintenance of physical operating levels requires replacement of services consumed, thereby requiring cash equal to the replacement cost of such services. When expenses are measured on the basis of replacement cost, the resulting income is a measure of distributable operating flows. This emphasis on maintenance of productive capacity was also incorporated into the Securities and Exchange Commission's replacement cost disclosure requirement (SEC, 1976).

8. According to an alternative view (Chambers, 1966; Sterling, 1972b), the impossibility of measuring a future event rules out the cash flow orientation; furthermore, the irrelevance of replacement cost of an asset now owned to future events involving that asset rules out replacement cost. Only present exit values are both relevant and objective. Even in cases of assets not likely to be sold in their present condition, exit values are relevant to (a) an appraisal of the firm's liquidity, (b) a judgment of its capacity to engage in indirect exchanges (Chambers, p. 101), and (c) an assessment of the risk a shareholder bears when he foregoes a larger sum of money (the price of a share) in order to hold an interest in a collection of assets (Sterling, p. 206).

Proponents of the decision-usefulness, decision model approach to accounting theory acknowledge certain implementation issues. Of particular importance are the issues associated with identification of the decision processes of users. First, there is the question of whether to rely on normative models or descriptive models. Sterling (1967) poses the choice as a fundamental dilemma:

If we are convinced that the receivers [decision makers] are using the wrong decision model, we have a dilemma. (1) We can transmit the information specified by their [decision makers'] wrong model which will yield right decisions only by chance. (2) We can transmit the information specified by the right model which will be irrelevant to their [decision makers'] model, and hence right decisions will result only by chance. (p. 106)

Differences of opinion about how to avoid the dilemma have arisen. Some have argued that we ought to focus on users and ignore the difficult, perhaps impossible, problem of determining when a decision model is right or wrong. This is what we have classified as the decision-usefulness, decision-*maker* approach (see Abdel-khalik, 1971) and is discussed below. Others have argued that the nature of the process requires that accountants become involved in the evaluation, refinement, and construction of decision models and then that they educate the receivers in the use of those models (see Sterling, 1970a, pp. 59ff). This is the decision-usefulness, decision *model* approach that is discussed in this section. Debate over decision-model versus decision-maker approaches to theory construction continues.

Another problem is how to deal with different user groups with different information wants (Revsine, 1973, pp. 5-8). For example, is there a conflict between the concern of short-term creditors with short-term ability to pay and the shareholders' concern with long-run payoffs? Does this possible difference imply the need for different measures of the same asset or liability, or only for recognition of the difference in reporting on short-term and long-term items in the balance sheet and related flow statements? Not only might different user groups want different data, but different individuals within one user group may differ in their decision processes in ways that call for different financial data. Issues of this type are still open.

Criteria Useful in Making Accounting Choices. Normative standards, or criteria necessary for information to be useful, serve a major supporting role in the decision-usefulness, decision model approach to accounting theory. Long before the decision-usefulness objective was explicitly adopted by accounting theorists, several qualities of financial information were recognized. For example, Sanders, Hatfield, and Moore (1938) emphasized conservatism and consistency of accounting methods. The AAA statement (1941) gave passing attention to objectivity, interperiod and intercompany comparability, and consistency. Moonitz (1961) included objectivity, consistency, and disclosure in his group-C postulates (imperatives). But none of those authors accepted the idea that criteria of useful information should be a cornerstone of their theories, because they did not emphasize the usefulness of information.

The first authors to advocate decision-usefulness also gave more attention to the qualities that were believed to make information useful, but they did not make the connection a very direct one. Thus, although Chambers (1955) was the first writer to emphasize the relevance of information, he did not develop the concept to the point of delineating the relevance of specific information to selected decisions. The AAA Supplementary Statement No. 8 (1955) underscored interperiod and intercompany comparability, recognized the importance of timeliness of reporting, and came close to the relevance criterion when it suggested that "the information to be conveyed should be selected on the basis of its significance to the investor . . . ." (p. 401). Staubus (1961) included a section on "Criteria for the Selection of Measurement Techniques" in which he discussed relevance, accessibility of evidence, cost, bias, and reliability, and ranked six measurement methods according to the criterion of relevance (p. 51).

The role of criteria of useful information in accounting theory achieved prominence in the mid-1960s with the work of the AAA Committee to Prepare a Statement of Basic Accounting Theory (1966). *A Statement of Basic Accounting Theory* (ASOBAT) began with a discussion of accounting objectives that specified information for making decisions, for directing and controlling an organization's resources, for the custodianship of resources, and for facilitating social functions and controls. It then turned to standards or criteria to be used in evaluating potential accounting information, the all-embracing criterion being usefulness. Other criteria were formulated by asking, "What characteristics should accounting information have in order to be useful?" Relevance, verifiability, freedom from bias, and quantifiability were suggested as standards. Consistency and uniformity were included among the second-tier "guidelines for communicating accounting information." Sterling (1967) provided further explication of these standards in a review of ASOBAT. Snavely (1967) modified the ASOBAT structure by adding understandability, "worth more than cost," timeliness, and significance (materiality), and by relating verifiability and freedom from bias under the heading of reliability. During the same period, Ijiri and Jaedicke (1966) contributed a discussion of the measurement of reliability, objectivity, and bias, while McDonald (1967) elaborated on those and other "feasibility criteria" in a treatment of dispersion, displacement, timeliness, cost, and correlation (of the accounting numbers with an attribute to be predicted). He also mentioned the all-inclusive criterion of net social benefit. Subsequent works making heavy use of the multiple-criteria approach were Accounting Principles Board Statement No. 4 (1970, Chapter 5), Staubus (1970), Sterling (1971), Kenley and Staubus (1972), Revsine (1973), and the Report of the Study Group on the Objectives of Financial Statements (1973).

It is crucial to observe the relationship between the decision-usefulness objective and the evolution of independent normative standards (such as comparability and objectivity) into a coherent set of criteria of useful information. First, the acceptance of the usefulness objective raised and emphasized the question, "What attributes of financial data make them useful to decision makers?" Without acceptance of the decision-usefulness objective, it seems unlikely that the multiple-criteria approach would have been developed to the extent that it has. Second, the normative concept that is generally recognized as primary — relevance to the decisions of users of financial statements — grew out of, and is dependent upon, the decision-usefulness objective.

Some criteria which have been advocated in contemporary literature for use in evaluating proposed accounting methods (information systems) and comparing competing proposals are presented in the following paragraphs.

Relevance. "Relevance" has been defined in a variety of ways, some of them rather vague and not helpful. For example, a general usage definition of "relevant," such as "bearing upon the matter at hand," may not be operational. Other possible definitions would make the term almost synonymous with usefulness, thus ruling it out as a criterion of usefulness. The current trend is to give relevance a specific meaning related to the potential role of information about an attribute (e.g., historical cost or net realizable value) of an object or event in the decision process. For example, "An attribute of an object or event is relevant to a decision if knowledge of it would help the decision-maker evaluate an outcome of one or more of the alternative courses of action under consideration" (Staubus, 1976). Or, "If a property is specified by a decision model, then a measure of that property is relevant (to that decision model)" (Sterling, 1972b, p. 199). Relevance is viewed as a necessary but not a sufficient condition for usefulness.

Reliability. Users of financial information prefer that it have a high degree of reliability. Reliability is that quality which permits users of data to depend upon it with confidence as representative of what it purports to represent. But reliable information is not necessarily useful. It could, for example, be reliable but unrelated to the use at hand. Several relatively general terms are often used as synonyms for, or to cover parts of, the concept of reliability. Thus, verifiability, objectivity, lack of bias, neutrality, and accuracy all are related to reliability. Like relevance, reliability (above some minimal level) is a necessary but not a sufficient condition for usefulness of data.

Other Criteria. Several writers have emphasized the value of a criterion that focuses attention on the receiving phase of the communication process. Understandability and readability are sometimes suggested.

Timeliness, including both frequency (interval) and lag (delay), is widely accepted as a criterion of useful information.

Optimal quantity and cost are closely related criteria. The literature of information economics stresses optimal partitioning and optimal aggregation. The possibility that certain information may not justify the cost of producing and utilizing it is generally recognized. Issues regarding cognitive processing levels (Revsine, 1970b; Driver and Mock, 1975) and their impact on decisions have also been recognized.

Many accountants believe that comparability is an important criterion for choosing among accounting methods. Others point out that the several types of comparability that are desirable may be included in relevance, reliability, or other criteria.

A number of accounting writers believe that the usefulness of accounting data in predicting phenomena of interest to decision makers is a criterion that should be used in evaluating alternative accounting proposals. Thus, Beaver, Kennelly, and Voss (1968) recommended the use of "predictive ability" as a criterion. Although these authors do not necessarily suggest that the accountant do the forecasting, other theorists have attempted to distinguish measurements from forecasts and have argued that the measurement function should be performed by the accountant and the forecasting function performed by the decision maker (Sterling, 1970a, 1972b; Revsine, 1973, pp. 40ff, 1975). That is, while it is clearly recognized that forecasts are relevant (indeed indispensable) to decisions, there have been some who have argued that the very nature of the market makes it necessary for the risk-bearing decision maker, as opposed to the accountant, to prepare the forecasts.

A review of the criteria discussed above will disclose that some criteria (e.g., relevance) are applicable primarily to the selection of attributes to be measured. Others (e.g., timeliness) play a significant role only in the choice of methods of data processing and communication. Still others may be important in almost any type of accounting issue. Finally, those who advocate the decision-usefulness, decision model approach have proposed as an ultimate criterion that the benefits yielded by accounting activities should exceed their costs.

Decision Makers

In the previous section we focused on decision *models*; we now shift to decision *makers* and review certain empirical research bearing upon various issues of financial reporting. Such research can be classified according to the level at which the behavior of decision makers is observed: the individual level or the aggregate market level. First, we focus on empirical research on individual behavior; the second section discusses aggregate market behavior.

Individual User Behavior. Empirical research involving observation of individual behavior as it relates to accounting information has ordinarily been associated with the term "behavioral accounting research" (BAR). The objective of BAR is to understand, explain, and predict aspects of human behavior relevant to accounting problems; that is, "to establish generalizations about human behavior that are supported by empirical evidence.... Behavioral science thus represents the systematic observation of man's behavior for the purpose of experimentally confirming specific hypotheses by reference to observable changes in behavior" (AAA, 1971b, p. 248).

Behavioral accounting research is relatively new. Devine's critical remarks in 1960 expose the failure of accountants to examine user behavior empirically before that time:

> Let us now turn to . . . the psychological reactions of those who consume accounting output or are caught in its threads of control. On balance, it seems fair to conclude that accountants seem to have waded through their relationships to the intricate psychological network of human activity with a heavy-handed crudity that is beyond belief. Some degree of crudity may be excused in a new discipline, but failure to recognize that much of what passes as accounting theory is hopelessly entwined with unsupported behavior assumptions is unforgivable. (p. 394)

Subsequent to Devine's remonstration, a growing literature in behavioral accounting has emerged. For example, Hofstedt (1976) provides evidence of the increasing share of the literature over the last ten years that has dealt with accounting and human behavior.

In this discussion, we are interested in empirical research on individuals as it relates to the selection of alternative accounting techniques in an external environment.

BAR studies ordinarily lack any agreed-upon basis by which their results may be assessed. Instead, BAR has been primarily concerned with studying the techniques of data collection and analysis; there has been little attempt to develop general theoretical formulations of problems or of hypotheses to be tested. The studies represent diverse attempts to understand, explain, and predict human behavior in an accounting setting without an agreed-upon universal theoretical perspective. As a consequence, BAR lacks a theoretical base to facilitate the selection of appropriate accounting procedures for individuals in economic decision making.

For these reasons it is difficult to classify BAR as it relates to external reporting. Nonetheless, some writers have attempted to develop systems of classification (Birnberg and Nath, 1967; Hofstedt, 1972; and Rhode, 1972). The most recent and probably the most exhaustive attempt was by Dyckman, Gibbins, and Swieringa (DGS, 1975). We have chosen one part of their classification to illustrate the general nature of studies conducted in BAR relating to the external reporting environment.[2] It should be emphasized that our discussion uses only the first section of the DGS paper and provides only a brief overview; readers should consult the original source for a more detailed discussion of the studies involved.

BAR studies may be divided into four general classes according to financial statement disclosure and the usefulness of financial statement data: (1) the adequacy of financial statement disclosure, (2) the usefulness of financial statement data, (3) attitudes about corporate reporting practices, and (4) materiality judgments.

In testing for the *adequacy of financial statement disclosure*, researchers have used many different strategies. For example, one strategy develops a description of a user's approach to financial statement analysis in order to evaluate the reasoning underlying that approach; it then assesses the implications of that approach and reasoning for various disclosure issues (e.g., Horngren, 1955, 1956, 1957). Another strategy focuses on certain interest groups and surveys their perceptions and attitudes about disclosure (e.g., Bradish, 1965; Ecton, 1969). A third strategy has been to determine the extent to which specific items of important information are disclosed in corporate annual reports, using a normative index of disclosure as a basis for assessment (e.g., Cerf, 1961; Singhvi and Desai, 1971; and Buzby, 1974).

A second set of studies has focused on the *usefulness of financial statement information* to investors in making resource allocation decisions. In one method, users of financial statements were asked to indicate the relative importance as information items of various factors in investment analysis (e.g., Baker and Haslem, 1973; Chandra, 1974). Another approach has been to try to determine whether financial statement data are used in decision making and whether their use is affected by other variables. This is done by creating a representation of a decision maker under quasi-laboratory conditions, and by studying the behavior of the subjects who make the decisions (e.g., Falk and Ophir, 1973a, 1973b; Libby, 1975a, 1975b). A final approach has been to attempt to measure the effectiveness of the communication of those data (e.g., Soper and Dolphin, 1964; Smith and Smith, 1971; Haried, 1972, 1973).

A third set of studies has attempted to measure the *attitudes and preferences of various groups toward current and proposed corporate reporting practices*. One approach has focused on preferences for alternative methods of accounting for specific transactions or events, such as a preference for a given form of business combination such as poolings of interest (Nelson and Strawser, 1970; Brenner and Shuey, 1972). Other attempts to measure attitudes have focused, more generally, on attitudes about how much information should be available, how much information is available, and how important given items are (Copeland, Francia, and Strawser, 1973; Godwin, 1975).

Another set of studies has focused on *materiality judgments* that affect financial reporting. Research on materiality judgments has generally attempted to determine what factors influence the collection, classification, and final summarization of accounting information (e.g., Woolsey, 1973; Dyer, 1973; Boatsman and Robertson, 1974; Pattillo, 1975; Pattillo and Siebel, 1973, 1974; Rose et al., 1970; Dickhaut and Eggleton, 1975). The major

---

[2] More specifically, the following five paragraphs are essentially a condensation of pp. 4-17 of the DGS paper. This area of research is important. However, our discussion is brief because of the recency of the DGS paper and its excellent synthesis of the area.

thrust of the research attempts to determine how much of a difference in accounting data is required before users perceive a difference.

It should be noted that these citations are not intended to be all-inclusive, nor is there any attempt to explain these studies and subsequent recommendations in any depth. However, this brief overview should provide a perspective on the ways in which some BAR specialists have conducted their empirical research in the behavioral area.

Aggregate Market-Level Research. The interest in decision usefulness extends not only to individual user responses to accounting variables, but to aggregate user response as well. To be sure, aggregate market behavior is a manifestation of individual action. However, according to proponents of market level research, there are factors that are difficult to simulate in individual level research (such as competing information sources, incentives, and user interactions) that are important in the study of groups; those factors thus prohibit a simplistic extension from the individual to the aggregate (e.g., see Gonedes, 1972; and Gonedes and Dopuch, 1974). Indeed, they may be so significant that theories about individual behavior and theories about market behavior become, in fact, theories about distinctly different things.[3] Therefore, some researchers believe that aggregating individual users' responses may not provide an apt description of market-wide user behavior.

Much early research regarding relations between accounting variables and market behavior has been based on the theory of capital market efficiency. The theory predicts that, on average, the abnormal return (return in excess of the equilibrium-expected return) to be earned from employing a set of extant information is zero (see Fama, 1970). This implies that an alteration in the information set will result in a prompt transition to a new equilibrium.

The theory is not specific with respect to the information set, and technical problems arise when it is admitted that the price actually reflects the underlying information (Grossman and Stiglitz, 1976). However, studies of accounting data have shown that upon release of those data, there is (at best) only a short-lived opportunity for abnormal returns. The prompt adjustment to a new equilibrium in conjunction with the dissemination of accounting data is consistent with the notion that those data are useful or possess pragmatic information content.[4] Following that logic, researchers have assessed the pragmatic information content of various accounting data by studying the timing of the incidence of abnormal returns. To do so, one must identify the relevant dates (i.e., when the data were externally available, and the length of the adjustment period to be observed) and a model by which to specify abnormal returns. One such model is the diagonal model attributed to Sharpe (1963). The diagonal model implies that the expected return on a particular security is a stable, linear function of the return on a portfolio of all securities in the market.[5] Operationally, the intercept and slope parameters are estimated by regressing an individual security return against the return on a market portfolio. Those parameters are then utilized to generate a prediction of the return on an individual security during a particular period. Any disparity between the actual return and the predicted return is considered to be abnormal.

---

[3] A discussion of selection of paradigms or research programs is provided in Chapter 4. For a recent review and analysis of aggregate market-level research, see Kaplan (1975).

[4] "Pragmatic information" refers to the reaction of individuals or groups to a sign or message. It is contrasted to "semantic information," which refers to the relation between a sign or message and the object or event that it signifies. For example, the message, "There is a fire in the building," will be said to have pragmatic information content if the receivers of that message react to it, if, say, someone calls the fire department — the reaction of receivers determines the measure of pragmatic information. By contrast, the semantic information of that same message is tested by observing the building to see whether or not there is in fact a fire. See Sterling (1970b, pp. 445-46, 453) for further discussion.

[5] Evidence on the applicability of this important model is provided by King (1966), Fama, Fisher, Jensen, and Roll (1969), and Gonedes (1973).

Since the mechanics of least squares regression produce, on average, a zero abnormal return, observation of large numbers of firms with abnormal returns coincidental with dissemination of accounting data is taken as an indicant of pragmatic information content.

A number of studies have been conducted along those lines. Ball and Brown (1968), Beaver (1968), and Gonedes (1974) consistently observed abnormal returns in conjunction with the announcement of the annual earnings number. May (1971) observed similar reactions to the quarterly announcement of firm earnings. In addition, anticipatory market reactions have been observed, suggesting the presence of competing information sources. Finally, the Gonedes study noted that the joint information implicit in several annual accounting numbers differed little from the information implicit in the earnings number by itself.

In other words, these studies are consistent with the notion that financial reports are useful. Stronger statements, though, must deal with questions about internal validity. The mere presence of an abnormal return coincidental with the publication of accounting earnings provides a somewhat tenuous basis from which to infer that the observed price movement was caused by the earnings signal. The principal basis upon which information content in attributed to accounting earnings is the rather impressive consistency with which abnormal returns concurrent with the publication of accounting earnings have been observed.

The early studies of the pragmatic information content of accounting earnings signals were extended to changes in accounting policy. Researchers investigated whether "artificial" accounting changes themselves affected security price behavior. The notion that security prices could be altered by mere bookkeeping phenomena devoid of economic import (or semantic information) dominated the literature prior to the early 1970s. However, studies of security price reactions to accounting policy changes by Kaplan and Roll (1972), Baskin (1972), Archibald (1972), and Ball (1972) generally indicated that alterations in reported earnings which were more or less devoid of present or future cash flow consequences could not produce significant long-lasting effects on stock prices. In addition, Sunder (1973) has provided evidence that changes in inventory valuation methods which reduce earnings but enhance future cash flows tend to be associated with increases in stock prices.[6]

The widespread belief that the mean and variance of an investment portfolio comprise the interesting parameters of investor choice led to use of the diagonal model in examining the extent to which accounting risk measures are associated with a security's contribution to portfolio variance.[7] A measure of that contribution is captured in the slope parameter (beta) of the diagonal model. Studies by Beaver, Kettler, and Scholes (1970), Gonedes (1973), Lev and Kunitzky (1974), and Bildersee (1975) indicated that accounting-based risk measures were contemporaneously correlated with beta. Thus, accounting risk measures appear to reflect whatever economic phenomena produce the variance in a portfolio return.

Further, Beaver, Kettler, and Scholes examined the usefulness of several accounting risk measures in predicting future values of beta; they concluded that accounting-based forecasts of beta were superior to naive forecasts based solely on present values of beta. Thus, accounting risk signals appear to have private value to an investor who seeks to predict the holding period risk of the portfolio. Perhaps more importantly, Beaver, Kettler, and Scholes suggested that security price research could be applied to the evaluation of certain accounting measurement issues. Specifically they posited that a simplified ordering of competing methods of accounting for common economic phenomena might be obtainable by observing the asso-

---

[6] Curiously, however, Sunder's data did not indicate significant decreases in stock prices in conjunction with inventory changes which increase earnings but reduce cash flow.

[7] Either quadratic utility functions over returns or normal return distributions are sufficient to demonstrate an exclusive interest in mean and variance. See Haley and Schall (1973, pp. 101-05).

ciations between earnings variability and beta, where earnings were defined using competing measurement methods.

Beaver and Dukes (1972) subsequently examined the associations between security prices and three competing definitions of accounting earnings: cash flow earnings, earnings with deferral of income taxes, and flow-through earnings. Their association metric was a variant of the Abnormal Performance Index (API) used by Ball and Brown (1968). The API measures the abnormal return that could have been earned from holding a portfolio for a specific number of periods culminating in the period of an earnings announcement. Securities comprising the portfolio are selected with hindsight provided by some earnings expectation model. More specifically, securities that subsequently have higher earnings than were originally forecasted are placed in one portfolio and securities with lower-than-forecasted earnings are placed in another. A positive API associated with the unexpectedly higher-than-forecasted earnings is alleged to be indicative of positive association between unexpected earnings and unexpected or abnormal price movements. Likewise, a negative API associated with a portfolio of securities with lower-than-forecasted accounting earnings is alleged to indicate positive association between unexpected earnings and prices.[8] Notice, however, that the entire line of research is conditional upon the particular model used to develop an expectation of accounting earnings. Beaver and Dukes utilized a variety of earnings expectations models to assess the associations between security prices (via the API metric) and their three competing definitions of earnings.[9] They concluded that deferral earnings generally possessed the highest association.

Since their findings were inconsistent with their expectations, Beaver and Dukes undertook a second study (1973) in which they treated various amounts of difference between tax expense and tax payable not as deferred charges or credits, but as a form of depreciation. They concluded that earnings numbers computed upon deduction of depreciation amounts exceeding reported depreciation tended to display the highest association with security prices.

To date, no other studies utilizing the API as a metric for ordering accounting alternatives have been forthcoming. As we discuss in the next chapter, questions have been raised whether the API indeed *can* be used to assess the association between price movements and accounting earnings. Further, Beaver and Dukes only *suggested* that their analysis provided information regarding the associations between expectations sequences and a price sequence; nevertheless, other questions have arisen regarding the wisdom of interpreting such analyses as assessments of the relative desirability of accounting alternatives. Those questions are also discussed in Chapter 3.

Information Economics

The applications of economics to accounting problems discussed in the previous sections utilized economic theory for the purpose of specifying what *kinds* of information were needed to make economic decisions. In this sense, information was not incorporated in the economic theory being applied. It was often treated as a free good, despite numerous references to a cost-benefit criterion. By contrast, the area of inquiry known as "information economics" treats information as a conventional economic commodity, the acquisition of which constitutes a problem of economic choice. That is, the product, information, is internalized in this approach to the formulation of the problem. Previous applications of economic theory had concerned themselves with the costs and prices of commodities other than information; this approach concerns itself with costs and prices of information as well.

In the following two sections we examine some insights provided by information economics. Initially, we review a

---

[8] It is important to note that the API is only a measure of information in a foreknowledge sense. For a discussion of the nature of foreknowledge, see Hirshleifer (1971).

[9] The importance of expectations models to this type of research is obvious. Several studies of the time series properties of accounting earnings have been undertaken. See Brown and Ball (1967), Beaver (1970), Ball and Watts (1972), Ball, Lev, and Watts (1976), Gonedes (1973), and Magee (1974).

model for information choice that focuses on a specific individual's demand for information. Then we extend the analysis into a domain of multiple individuals.

The Single Individual Case

In the single individual case, we view the demand for information in terms of its ability to improve the quality of the ultimate choice in some choice problem that the individual faces. Put another way, the demand for information is a derived demand; information is valued because it improves the quality of decisions.

To analyze a demand for information, we posit a basic choice problem that an individual must resolve. He must select one action from a set of at least two available alternative actions. The precise outcome that will follow selection of any specific action is not generally known. Rather, a set of possible outcomes is envisioned; only one will occur, but precisely which one is uncertain.

If the individual's preferences are represented by the expected utility hypothesis, however, we have a precise representation of how his choice will be made. Each possible action gives rise to a lottery of outcomes, in which each possible outcome is assigned an action-conditional probability. (These probability assignments may be exogenously specified, as in the von Neumann-Morgenstern [1947] axiomatization, or endogenously specified, as in the Savage [1954] axiomatization.) Each possible outcome is also assigned a utility measure. The expected utility of each action is then merely the expected value of the outcome-utility measure. One action is preferred to another if and only if its expected utility measure is greater than that of the other.

Information can now be readily introduced into the analysis. The motive for acquiring information is to learn about what outcomes will be associated with what actions. Thus, with outcome possibilities assessed with a probability measure, performing an experiment or producing an accounting report is viewed in terms of providing a random outcome whose observance leads to (Bayesian) revision of the original outcome probabilities.

A decision of what information to acquire, then, is viewed in terms of a two-stage lottery or gamble. First, the information source or accounting system will produce some signal or message. Precisely what signal will be produced is uncertain and probabilities are assigned to each possibility. Second, following signal observance, outcome probabilities are revised and a conditional best action is selected, thereby resulting in an outcome lottery. In turn, the expected utility of the specific source is the joint expectation of the utility of the outcomes associated with the conditional best actions. One reporting system is preferred to another if and only if its expected utility measure is higher than that of the other. Moreover, at zero cost, less information would never be preferred to more.[10] (Further note that the cost of the information is accounted for by appropriately adjusting the outcomes that may materialize.)[11]

We have, in other words, a specific description of how information is used (Bayesian revision) and a specific criterion for designing an information or accounting system (subjective expected utility maximization). One limitation of this approach results from the traditional economic assumption of consistent, rational choice behavior.

The Multi-Individual Case

Now consider a situation in which a number of heterogeneous individuals have a demand for information, such as public financial reports. Analyzing this case in an economic manner pushes us into the realm of welfare economics. Two questions emerge. First, given that we treat information as an economic good, is there any reason to worry about regulating its production, or can we treat the multiple-user situation in a conventional market setting? Second, if we cannot rely on a market solution and thus must consider regulatory in-

---

[10] This is Blackwell's theorem. See Marschak and Radner (1972) or Demski and Feltham (1976).

[11] The basic work in information economics is attributed to Jacob Marschak. See Marschak and Radner (1972). Application to accounting issues is discussed in Demski (1972), Feltham (1972), and Demski and Feltham (1976).

tervention, what is the nature and extent of the regulatory activity that should be employed?

The Regulation Question. To shed light on the first question, we initially review the economic arguments for intervention in a market economy. We then apply these standard concerns to an examination of the properties of information.

If we adopt a normative social choice criterion of Pareto optimality, to be consistent with this criterion, an allocation of resources should be interpersonally efficient in the sense that no reallocation can strictly improve one group's well-being without harming some other group's well-being. Quite naturally, then, for intervention or regulation to be an issue, a laissez faire determination of the production and consumption of goods and services must provide an allocation of resources that is not efficient.[12] Under the usually assumed individual, firm, and market conditions, however, the laissez faire solution is, in fact, efficient.[13] That is, a further increase in any group's well-being can occur only at the expense of some other group. Under these conditions, there is no incentive for regulation at this point.

That pleasant situation is altered, however, if we recognize the possibility in interdependencies that are not properly mitigated by the prevailing market structure. That is, if the market system fails to incorporate all of the interaction effects of resource allocations, efficiency is not assured. Several examples of these interdependencies (or externalities) exist: consumption or production by one may pollute another; increasing returns to scale may be present; or the extreme case of a pure public good (where acquisition by one makes the identical amount costlessly and automatically available to all) may be the issue at hand.

The difficulty in such situations is that individual decision agents do not internalize the effect of their choices on others. A polluter, for example, does not naturally account for the effect his pollution has on others — a fact stressed by recent concern for social accounting programs. A more extreme case of externalities is the phenomenon of a public good, that is, one available to a single consumer only if the producer provides the good to all members of the society. Such goods cannot be appropriated by some individuals to the exclusion of others. Thus, a price cannot be charged for the good that will effectively reflect differing individual preferences for the good. For example, consider national defense. The protective benefits of national defense are enjoyed by all members of society; the benefit that an individual receives from national defense is not reflected in a price he is willing to pay, since he receives the benefit of national defense production whether he pays or not. Thus, private producers of public goods are not able to incorporate in their decision making the positive effects of production on nonpurchasers (thereby creating the suspicion of under-production). Without such internalization, market-based solutions may not be efficient and the question of regulation arises.[14]

Only the *question* arises, however. Existence of an externality effect (or its public good extreme) is not a sufficient condition for intervening in the laissez faire solution. Establishing a corrective mechanism will be costly, and those costs are one of the determinants of whether intervention is desirable. Similarly, the affected parties may be naturally motivated to resolve their differences privately (e.g., merger). In other words, intervention is a vastly deeper issue than mere observation of a potential inefficiency.

Next we consider whether externalities

---

[12] A second argument for intervention is based on "ethical" or "humanitarian" grounds; in such a case the distribution of goods and services is at issue and, strictly speaking, we address the question of movement from one efficient point to another. Of course, public good and externality aspects are also involved in the distribution question.

[13] See Arrow and Hahn (1971), Debreu (1959), Henderson and Quandt (1971), Malinvaud (1972), or Quirk and Saposnik (1968) for further discussion.

[14] Analyses are available in the literature. See Due and Friedlaender (1973), Henderson and Quandt (1971), and Malinvaud (1972).

are likely to be associated with information in an otherwise classical economy.

Analysis indicates that financial accounting information shares much in common with the more traditional examples of externalities. Its use by one does not necessarily preclude subsequent enjoyment by others. Once produced, an annual report or newspaper may be read by numerous individuals. And in the extreme, its value to any specific individual may be completely independent of who else possesses it.[15] Coupling the possibility of nondestruction in consumption with the facts that production of information is, by nature, a risky activity (uncertainty is a necessary condition for information to have value), and that prevailing property rights may make the total benefit from production not completely appropriable by the producer, we are led to conclude that, without intervention, too little information will be produced (see Arrow, 1962, or Due and Friedlaender, 1973). This is one of the standard arguments for such activities as patent laws and disclosure policies. Of course, we must temper this argument by recognizing the costliness of intervention (see Demsetz, 1969).

The possible difficulties are, however, further complicated if one admits that the distribution of information across individuals is also an important determinant of the consumption schedules ultimately enjoyed by each. That is, if everyone had the same information, blackmail, sign-stealing in baseball, and code-breaking in war would be unnecessary. Other illustrations are provided by moral hazard and adverse selection phenomena. In the phenomenon of moral hazard, two parties make an insurance agreement. But the observed event on which the insurance is based is an outcome that is *jointly* determined by nature and the insured. That, in turn, reduces the insured's decision-making incentives (as in cost-plus contracting), and we thereby arrive at insurance contracts that are less efficient in risk sharing than would be the case with better information.[16] This is, in fact, a special case of the problem of incomplete markets (see Radner, 1974).

Adverse selection, on the other hand, occurs when private information provides a basis for self-selection. Individuals with "bad" used automobiles have an incentive to misrepresent their autos in the used auto market as "good" because a buyer's information about the quality of the auto is inferior to that of the seller. Indeed, a potential seller of a "good" used automobile may be unable to attract a price that is consistent with the auto's quality because of the "bad" autos that are misrepresented in the market. In a similar fashion, sickness-prone people have a strong incentive to apply for health insurance. In turn, countervailing institutions such as advertising or independent appraising arise; intervention may be sought, as in the case of licensing or mandatory health insurance (see Akerlof, 1970; Hirshleifer, 1973; and Spence, 1973).

These distributive effects associated with information differences across individuals have begun to be examined in an investment setting. The work of Hirshleifer (1971) and Fama and Laffer (1971), (and continuing with that of Gonedes, Dopuch, and Penman, 1975; Jaffe, 1974; Kihlstrom and Mirman, 1975; Marshall, 1974; Ng, 1975; Radner, 1974; and Wilson, 1974), provide examples. A major implication of these related explorations is that it is possible to have overproduction as well as underproduction of information. For example, in a pure exchange economy with homogeneous beliefs, information production merely redistributes the wealth among the individuals; no social gain whatever is produced. Indeed, it is also possible to construct examples where — due to the distributive effects — all individuals are unanimous in opposing the production of information (see Marshall, 1974; and Ng, 1975).

---

15 Gonedes (1975) formulates a problem where the private value of information is independent of how many use it; with costly production this leads to a monopolistic producer. Under conditions that allow for exclusion of nonpurchasers he is then able to characterize efficient production and use conditions.

16 See Kihlstrom and Pauly (1971) and Spence and Zeckhauser (1971) for analysis of the effect of basing insurance contracts on incomplete knowledge of the insured's behavior.

Alternative Theory Approaches

In summary, externally reported financial information is a public good and this introduces the possibility — as is true with other public goods — of *under*production (in this case, underproduction of information). On the other hand, distributive effects of information differences introduce the possibility of *over*production of information. Thus, putting these two phenomena together, it is not at all clear whether inefficiency results in a market setting. In theory, the answer is clearly affirmative. But in a real-world situation, we simply do not know. No research, to our knowledge, has systematically addressed that question.

The Normative Criterion Question. With inefficiency an open question, discussion of intervention and regulation is, of course, somewhat premature. Furthermore, issues of "fairness" are apparently also involved. Blackmail is generally frowned upon in the sense that an "unfair" distribution of information produces the transfer of wealth. Similar thoughts are expressed about "unfair" advertising, incomplete candor in real estate and security sales, and insider trading. (Of course, allowing insider trading may be a least cost method of producing the information.) In any event, the precise motivation for intervention is ambiguous at this point.

Suppose, however, that we face a situation in which the market allocation is inefficient, or is the product of an undesirable initial allocation of resources (including access to information), or both. Some form of intervention will be pursued in order to achieve a more desirable, efficient allocation. The question then involves what criterion should govern this policy decision.

Quite simply, the problem is one of finding a criterion to guide nonmarket allocations. Cost-benefit analysis is a popular term for a large subset of such activity. The concept is deceptively appealing: the "costs" and "benefits" are tallied and an alternative with maximal gain is selected. Unfortunately, the concept of employing some well-defined objective function is largely illusory in that it runs afoul of the Arrow Paradox. This concept is further discussed in Chapter 3.

In summary, the information economics approach offers an explicit individual-demand-based analysis of accounting policy questions. Rationality is the major assumption employed. This approach provides a means for examining whether regulatory intervention (i.e., rules specifying form and content) is desirable in an external reporting context. The power of the approach is in isolating general relationships and effects of alternative scenarios. At present, however, the approach is still too general to provide definitive answers to existing policy issues.

Summary

In this chapter we have identified and classified three prominent approaches to the construction of accounting theory: (1) classical ("true income" and inductive) models; (2) decision-usefulness; and (3) information economics. Our synopsis clearly indicates many differences in problems addressed, assumptions made, and analytic methods employed across the various approaches. While the differences are fundamental and starkly visible, and while the issues and conclusions are often inconsistent among alternative approaches, theorists have had little success in reconciling these differences or in persuading critics that their unique structure is superior to others. Issues are continually recycled and closure appears to be no nearer.

This situation naturally requires explanation, and in the next two chapters this statement endeavors to provide it. In Chapter 3 we explore conceptual issues that arise in the specific accounting environment. As we will see, these issues are currently unresolved and consequently serve to preclude theory closure at this time. Worse still, many of these issues are not amenable to a solution using the mode of logic and rigorous analysis upon which theorists have long relied. In Chapter 4 we generalize our Chapter 3 discussion and offer a philosophy of science interpretation of the continuing disagreement (recognizing, of course, that competing models exist). That chapter provides insight into the nature of the pervasive basic problem that makes theory progress in accounting — and other disciplines — such an arduous task.

Appendix

This Appendix contains analyses of the writings of Sweeney, MacNeal, Paton and Littleton, and Alexander, which are intended to supplement the discussion in Chapter 2. Full reference to the works cited in the Appendix will be found in the bibliography.

Henry W. Sweeney
Stabilized Accounting (1936)

Sweeney's other writings include "Maintenance of Capital" (1930), "Stabilized Appreciation" (1932), "Capital" (1933), and "Income" (1933).

Sweeney was much influenced by Fisher. His decision on the dichotomy between capital and income is predicated on the intrinsic (i.e., economic) attributes of each notion. Sweeney aligns himself with Fetter in the famous Fisher-Fetter argument over whether the inclusion of capital gains in income is double counting.

The closest that Sweeney comes to appealing to the needs of users is his statement that "... the true function of accounting is, or should be, to summarize financial data in such a way as to enable a maximum of helpful information regarding an enterprise to be obtained at a minimum of cost" (1936, p. 199). Only in the Preface to *Stabilized Accounting* does he specify the users: primarily business management, but also the owners, bankers, federal and state tax authorities, and the general financial public. Truthfulness is the controlling tenet, but Sweeney does not show how truthfulness leads to better decisions.

The entire thrust of Sweeney's argument is of the "true income" school, notwithstanding isolated appeals to the needs of various users.

Kenneth MacNeal
Truth in Accounting (1939)

MacNeal's work is predominantly of the "true income" school, although elements of a decision model approach recur. The decision model is implicit.

Here is the epitome of the "true income" argument:

There is one correct definition of profits in an accounting sense. A profit is an increase in net wealth. A loss is a decrease in net wealth. This is an economist's definition. It is terse, obvious, and mathematically demonstrable.... The function of accounting is to record, collate, and present economic truths.... (p. 295)

MacNeal, however, is not a partisan of discounted present value. The truth, he says, should be "unmodified by future improbabilities, probabilities, [and] even certainties" (p. 46). His preference is for "economic value," which he translates as market prices in a free, competitive, broad, and active market (Chapter 7). In the case of inventories, market price would seem to be selling price, yet MacNeal ordinarily is satisfied by the use of replacement cost as a surrogate. In general, he recommends market prices for "marketable assets," imputed economic values (e.g., appraisals or replacement cost) for "reproducible, nonmarketable assets," and original cost less amortization or depletion for "nonreproducible, nonmarketable assets" (Chapter 9). These choices are evidently a concession to the practical problems of measurement.

Notwithstanding his dominant true income orientation, MacNeal frequently refers to the information which stockholders require in order to know the worth of their shares (Chapters 9, 10, and 14, and p. 2). Moreover, "Creditors have the same right to know the true status of a company as do stockholders. If the facts are misrepresented, creditors are deprived of a sound basis for deciding whether to extend or withhold credit. The same reasoning applies with even more force to depositors and policy holders" (p. 221).

The use of discounted present values, contends MacNeal, "deceives stockholders and creditors, and deprives them of a truthful basis of present fact upon which to base their own estimates of the future" (p. 146). The requirements of managers are mentioned (pp. 180-81). Thus, MacNeal's construct, while an appeal to truth as economic values, nonetheless reflects the various uses to which truth is put by diverse readers. MacNeal evinces a greater explicit concern for the lot of specific users than does Sweeney. Neither author links truth to users' specific decision models.

W. A. Paton and A. C. Littleton
An Introduction to Corporate Accounting Standards (1940)

To many readers, this monograph might defy classification as either deductive or inductive. Insofar as it represents a deductive argument, one would opt for the decision model approach. Yet notwithstanding the ostensibly normative vein in which the argument is sometimes conveyed, the frequent use of the indicative mood recalls the Littletonian alloy of deduction and induction — a massaged generalization. An example: "The accountant . . . deals primarily with the administration of the affairs of the continuing business institution and accordingly emphasizes the flow of costs and the interpretation of assets as balances of unamortized costs" (pp. 10-11). Do the authors imply that this is what the accountant *should* do, or only what he *does* do? Are they content with generalizing from practice and interpolating an integrated rationalization, or is it coincidence that their explanation of proper accounting largely coincides, at least in terms of result, with what accounting is? On at least some points (e.g., purchase discounts and "cost or market"), the authors recommend procedures that appear to depart from settled practice. It is worth noting that one of the reviewers of the monograph, a leading practitioner, said that it "attempts to build a coherent structure on a philosophical foundation, rather than to discover any coherence in the field of accounting as it is" (Wilcox, 1941, p. 75). In that day, practice was diverse, and practitioners were not accustomed to coherent structures. It is doubtful that a coherent structure any more faithful to then extant practice could have been produced.

The decision model, if any, is implicit. The authors go no further than, "The purpose of accounting is to furnish financial data concerning a business enterprise, compiled and presented to meet the needs of management, investors, and the public" (headnote, p. 1). Although they underscore the importance of the absentee owner, their discussion of the possible uses to which current value information might be put is related to the decisions made by management (e.g., pricing and replacement).

Transaction-based price aggregates dominate the analysis. Few exceptions in the accounts and in the body of the financial statements are tolerated. "The emphasis on the cost basis . . . rejects the proposition that periodic revaluation has a settled place within the regular accounting framework" (pp. 125-26); that is a disturbing tautology. Current values and general price-level data, although impermissible in the body of the financial statements, may nonetheless appear in supplementary schedules or reports. These constitute "interpretive" information in the Littletonian sense.

An argument frequently given (pp. 123, 135, 141) in support of historical cost is the constraint imposed by legal requirements. At one place, the term "contractual earnings" is used, evidently connoting the notion of earnings contemplated by contracting parties, or perhaps by legislation and judicial opinion. The authors do not argue for an idealized notion of income, and they are conscious of institutional boundaries.

The authors' persistently positivist form of expression confounds the reader. Another example: "From the point of view of the managers and owners of the enterprise the cost incurred is regularly the significant measure of operating effort . . ." (p. 23). "Ought to be" or "is"? While the stated purpose of accounting, quoted above, is couched in the indicative mood, the authors elsewhere state that accounting "must represent a practical tool of business and finance, competent to meet the legitimate needs of managers, investors, government, and the public at large" (pp. 4-5). Fulsomely normative.

Perhaps the clearest expression of the authors' view of their mission appears on page 4:

A statement of accounting standards should represent an integrated conception of the function of accounting as a means of expressing the financial facts of business in a significant manner. It must inevitably embody some conflict with existing accounting practices, since existing practice is in conflict with itself at a hundred points. It should avoid any appearance of encouraging violations of existing law, but it need not accept as good accounting all definitions, policies, and practices which legislators and courts have added to the accounting structure.

In vivid contrast to MacNeal's work, the Paton and Littleton monograph was evidently written so as not to annoy the practitioner audience. At that time, the American Accounting Association was attempting to replace rivalry by collaboration in its relations with the American Institute of Accountants, as the AICPA was then called. Copies of the monograph were distributed without charge to members of both bodies, and the authors clearly sought to achieve a maximum favorable impact on practitioners without sacrificing their principles. This motive could explain the indicative mood.

Much of the writing is Paton's but all the ideas are not. Price aggregates, and the dominant "interpretation" theme of the final chapter are pure Littleton. Yet most of Paton's ideas find expression in the monograph.

Notwithstanding the authors' frequent reference to "standards," even in the title of their monograph, their approach cannot fairly be characterized as falling in the same class as ASOBAT. Paton and Littleton enumerate measurement rules which are assertedly predicated on the several concepts, conventions, and assumptions set forth in Chapter 2. If there is a pervasive standard (i.e., normative standard), it is dependability, which is frequently invoked in defense of traditional historical cost. In fact, the authors did not undertake to enumerate standards, but instead to lay the groundwork for a future exposition of standards.

Sidney S. Alexander
"Income Measurement in a Dynamic Economy" (1950)
(revised by D. Solomons in *Studies in Accounting Theory*, 1962)

Alexander's attitude toward the existence of "true income" is not easily categorized. Throughout the essay he repeatedly stresses that the utility of a given income system must be assessed in relation to the intended use for the resultant measurements (see Baxter and Davidson, 1962, pp. 130, 146, and 164). This strongly hints of the decision model, rather than the true income, approach to income theory. However, in several places in the essay, Alexander makes statements which suggest that in theory at least an ideal income concept does indeed exist. For example:

> ... we must find out whether economic income is an ideal from which accounting income differs only to the degree that the ideal is practically unattainable, or whether economic income is inappropriate even if it could conveniently be measured. (p. 159)

In summary, Alexander probably falls somewhere between the "true income" and decision alternatives.

Chapter 3

Criticisms of Present Theory Approaches

This committee has looked for reasons why none of the alternative theory approaches discussed in Chapter 2 has risen to a position of singular prominence in contemporary accounting thought. None of them has been left unchallenged; indeed, a steady stream of counterarguments and criticisms appears to have prevented any of the approaches from gaining a clear majority of accounting theory students as supporters.

Many prominent criticisms of alternative accounting theory approaches were clearly discernible in 1966, when the Association's most recent major theoretical document, *A Statement of Basic Accounting Theory*, was written. Since then, additional points of dissatisfaction with one or more of these approaches have appeared in the literature. Further, some of the traditional criticisms have received renewed support.

In this chapter we survey some of the contemporary points of conflict that arise in the accounting literature. Clearly, each point is not shared by all critics. In the aggregate, however, they apparently serve to preclude a meaningful consensus regarding financial accounting theory. Our survey is not intended to be exhaustive; however, it should convey the fundamental levels at which objections to proposed theoretical approaches are raised. Six different issues are summarized in this chapter: (1) the general problem of relating theories to practice; (2) the allocation problem; (3) the problem with normative standards; (4) the problem with basing accounting theories on securities price research; (5) the problem of cost-benefit considerations in accounting theories; and (6) the danger in assuming that more information is preferable to less. Collectively these points of conflict illustrate why no theoretical approach has yet achieved dominant acceptance within the accounting community.

The Problem of Relating Theories to Practice

Apparently, accountants expect or hope that the process of accounting theorizing will lead to a sufficient and compelling basis for specifying the content of external financial reports. However, even if a single theoretical approach should rise to prominence, many of the day-to-day issues faced by practicing accountants and auditors probably would persist. For example, in many proposed theories, issues of materiality would remain issues. Furthermore, to the extent accountants fail to perceive and accept limits to the practical coverage provided by a theory, all theoretical approaches are apt to be controversial because of the gaps they leave in guiding practical applications.

One possible source of practical dissatisfaction with a theory is its lack of coverage or breadth. For example, some expositions of inductive theories have leaned heavily on statements to the effect that assets are valued at historical cost, and have neglected those assets, such as cash and receivables, which are not customarily valued at cost, along with all liabilities. Another example is the case of the theorist who limits his concern with flows to income statement changes to the exclusion of changes in working capital, even though statements of changes in financial position are acknowledged to be a vital part of practical accounting. Theories with such gaps are bound to be perceived as inadequate for yielding the answers that practitioners seek.

Another practical problem with theories is that they do not always recognize alternative possible features of the environment and specify how to deal with them. This "weakness" of theories may be associated with unrealistic assumptions made by the theory, such as competitive equilibrium, zero transaction costs, immaterial fringe acquisition costs of commodities and services, complete markets, zero costs of producing and utilizing accounting data, stability of the monetary measuring unit, homogeneity of decision models among members of a user group, and mutuality of interests of owners and managers. Observed inconsistencies between such assumptions (and the resulting simplifications of the theories) and the environment in which accountants work may cause practitioners to lose faith in all theories.[1]

It is not clear that theorists can overcome the problem of incomplete specification by adding realism to their assumptions; the real world is very complex and complexity is also a weakness in a theory. A complex theory may be more difficult to apply, and therefore its popularity among practitioners will be lessened. For example, the evaluation of information systems in accordance with the approach of information economics may escape the criticisms of narrow coverage or inadequate provision for variations in the environment. But the complexity of the information evaluation task, as outlined in the information economics section of the previous chapter, may well cause many accountants to avoid it. Similarly, if a theorist specifies a large number of normative criteria that an accounting method should meet, the practitioner may not be able to make the complex set of trade-offs that are required to apply the theory. Perhaps the notion of an optimal quantity of data that accountants should provide to users in order to maximize the net value of information can be adapted to apply to the amount of detailed specifications in an accounting theory. But differences among accountants in their tolerance (or desire) for detailed guidance are bound to subject any theory to criticism by some of its users. An admirably simple accounting theory is not likely to yield immediate and unequivocal answers to all accounting decision situations. To the extent that accounting theories are evaluated on these criteria, no theory is likely to be wholly satisfactory. That is one possible explanation for the lack of general acceptance of any theoretical approach.

The Allocation Problem

Most of the alternative approaches to specifying the content of external financial reports rely heavily upon allocation processes. Even if allocation procedures are avoided in formulating the general framework of a proposal, they are frequently introduced at a more specific level. Thomas (1969, 1974) has argued that the allocation problem is an inherently insoluble one that pervades most external reporting proposals.

The most serious objection to allocation techniques is that many are inherently arbitrary. A familiar example of arbitrary allocation in U.S. accounting principles is the oft-quoted description of depreciation accounting published by the AICPA in 1953: "*Depreciation accounting* is a system of accounting which aims to distribute the cost or other basic value of tangible capital assets, less salvage (if any), over the estimated useful life of the unit (which may be a group of assets) in a systematic and rational manner. It is a process of allocation, not of valuation . . . ." The absence of any guidance as to the meaning of "rational" in this context has enabled accountants to defend widely varying time-patterns of depreciation. Many accountants agree with Thomas that this is a weakness in those theoretical statements reflecting U.S. accounting principles, such as *ARS No. 7* (Grady, 1965, pp. 148-51).

The extent of dissatisfaction with accounting procedures involving allocations appears to vary widely. One probable reason that dissatisfaction varies is that the meanings attributed to the term "allocation" vary. Some accountants limit their application of the term to cases in which one monetary amount is split among several accounts or periods without direct reference to either physical or monetary evidence as a basis for the split. Others extend the term to such cases as splitting rent among departments on the basis of floor

---

[1] The question of whether a theory should be evaluated on the basis of the realism of its assumptions in addition to its predictive power remains unsettled. Cf. Friedman (1953), Nagel (1963), Samuelson (1963), and Carsberg, Arnold, and Hope (1977).

space occupied, or even to charging the salary of an employee to the department in which he worked. In the view of many accountants, there is a vast difference in the arbitrariness of these various procedures. Nevertheless, it seems safe to say that there is widespread dissatisfaction with those procedures that appear to fall at the more arbitrary end of the spectrum.

The fact that an allocation technique is arbitrary does not mean that it is indefensible. On the contrary, in Thomas' own words:

> The difficulty is more subtle: for each situation in which allocation is contemplated, there is a variety of possible allocation methods, *each* of which could be defended. The allocation problem arises because there is no conclusive way to choose one method in preference to all others, except arbitrarily. (1974, p. 2)

Thomas illustrates at length the arbitrariness of various classes of allocation techniques and the inability to defend these techniques rigorously to the exclusion of available alternatives. Since conclusive selection is impossible, endless argumentation ensues. While some may dispute Thomas' conclusion that (given our current state of knowledge) allocation techniques are totally arbitrary, at a minimum it is apparent that such allocations give rise to vexing controversies.[2] The irresolvability of these allocation-induced controversies explains, at least in part, why theoretical approaches in which allocation plays an integral role have not gained widespread acceptance.

The Difficulty with Normative Standards

As discussed in Chapter 2, some theories of external reporting incorporate normatively posited standards that provide a basis for choosing information to be included in external reports. Such standards include objectivity, verifiability, and timeliness, among others. One important characteristic of some of these standards is that they refer to properties that are intrinsic to the accounting numbers themselves; they are not inferred from the personal preferences of the individual users of accounting data. As a consequence, the relationship between the proposed normative standards and the individual preferences of decision makers is indirect. Since normative standards that are divorced from individual preferences cannot *completely* surrogate those preferences, the imposition of such standards presents serious difficulties. Specifically, if we assume that an accounting system should be designed to maximize, say, the expected utility of the users of accounting data, the data chosen to conform to imposed standards will not consistently lead to that result.

Consider an individual user of accounting data whose preferences can be represented by the expected utility hypothesis; that is, he guides his behavior in a manner that results in maximum expected utility. Further assume that our individual uses accounting information to make more than one type of economic decision. Since each type of decision incorporates potentially diverse dimensions, each distinct decision category may result in emphasis on different properties of the financial phenomena at hand. For example, if accounting policy makers adopted objectivity as a criterion for selecting information to be reported to this individual, the resultant information system might actually maximize the expected utility for one type of decision made by the individual. That is, the preferences of the individual in the context of a specific type of decision may require that objectivity be the dominant criterion in construct-

---

[2] An interesting manifestation of the allocation dilemma arises when we attempt to define the concept of income in an uncertainty setting. Following the Hicksian tradition, we think in terms of temporal wealth measurement. Yet future cash flows, in an uncertainty setting, are characterized by probability distributions. In a complete embracing of state-indexed commodity production and exchange (e.g., Debreu 1959), however, no difficulty is encountered. Each possible distribution of future cash flows has a known market price and wealth calculations are straightforward. But difficulties emerge if we do not have access to these market prices—that is, if the markets are incomplete. Here the traditional allocation dilemma again emerges, both in terms of "assigning" period by period components of the cash flow as well as (recognizing state dependence) in interpreting the resultant income measure. However, market incompleteness and the resultant allocation dilemma, not uncertainty *per se*, is the cause of the difficulty.

ing the system from which he obtains information input to his decision process. However, if the same individual uses the same information in the context of a different type of decision, his preferences may require that objectivity not be the dominant criterion in the second context.

Furthermore, no two decision problems are identical. New environmental dimensions can suddenly materialize even in recurring, somewhat standardized decision areas. In other words, the process of defining a "type of decision" for which a specified normative standard will be appropriate cannot be expected to be stable as environmental changes occur. As a consequence, there is no guarantee that a normative standard consistent with utility maximization on one occasion will necessarily lead to utility maximization in an altered decision environment. (Indeed, the setting becomes more perverse if we allow the individual's preferences to shift over time, and we have no basis for assuming that this is a rare occurrence.)[3]

In a more realistic portrayal of the reporting environment, the problems of using normative standards to specify the information system are complicated even further by the obvious existence of many individual users. Observation of human behavior suggests that the preferences of individuals are diverse. To cite a few examples, some individuals may value prosperity highly, while others strive merely for a "comfortable" living standard; some pursue increments to wealth under highly risky conditions, while others will not; and some have a more highly developed social conscience than do others. Since individuals in a multi-person setting have diverse preferences, no single set of standards for external reporting is likely to be consistent with those diverse preferences.[4] Moreover, the question of how diverse individuals would or should specify public reporting policies is largely open. And we simply do not know the relationship between any set of standards and such group-level choice behavior.

Thus whether viewed in a single- or multi-person setting, normative standards do not appear to offer a noncontroversial basis for theory building or policy choice.

Difficulties in Interpreting Security Price-Behavior Research

As we noted in Chapter 2, considerable empirical research based on the efficient market hypothesis has attempted to discern how investors, viewed in the aggregate, use accounting measures. Briefly, that research tries to interpret the contemporaneous association of information flow with unexplained variations in rates of return on securities as an indication of "information content." Two caveats are, however, important when we undertake to interpret these types of studies.[5]

---

[3] Of course, one might argue that, in the ideal case, the standards will be rich enough to "work" in all settings. However, this cannot be the case because the necessary and sufficient conditions for such a state of affairs, as specified by Blackwell's theorem (see Marschak and Radner, 1972), preclude any such universal set of standards.

This argument is presented by Demski (1973a). Its essence is as follows. Without loss of generality, assume the policy maker is faced with choosing between two accounting alternatives, η' and η''. Further assume that η' and η'' can be compared in terms of fineness, wherein η' is said to be as fine as η'' if η' provides as much information as η'' and possibly more. For example, deferral of income taxes would appear to be as fine as nondeferral, since deferral contains as much information as nondeferral, and perhaps more. If η' and η'' are costless, it is clear that η' as fine as η'' is sufficient to induce the policy maker to desire η' at least as much as η''. However, η' as fine as η'' is also a necessary condition for η' to be at least as desirable as η''. (This is the essence of Blackwell's theorem.) Therefore, any standards which are used to surrogate preferences must also surrogate fineness.

The difficulty is that fineness is not a complete relation—some information systems are not comparable in terms of fineness. For example LIFO and FIFO probably cannot be compared on a fineness dimension. Since fineness is incomplete, there are cases in which standards cannot possibly surrogate fineness and, in turn, preferences. Therefore, standards surrogating preferences are, in general, an impossibility.

[4] Some of the objections raised against the decision-usefulness, decision model approach are based on this point. Specifically, that approach seeks to provide information specified by the decision model of a certain category of users. But this ignores the potential redistributive effects on other users whose information desires are excluded from the analysis.

[5] Some, such as Thomas (1974, pp. 89-91), reject all such evidence on grounds that the individual behaviors that are aggregated in market statistics are them-

First, whether we interpret the studies as attempts to assess *consequences* or *desirability* of measurement method changes, we nevertheless confront the traditional experimental concerns of internal and external validity (as we do in all empirical studies). Most clearly, the tests are based on controlling for all "obvious" return factors (such as market-wide phenomena, arrival of other information, and risk changes); the tests are therefore limited by our ability to identify and allow for the effect of such factors. Whether a correlated variable is overlooked remains problematic (see Gonedes and Dopuch, 1974).

Second, when one interprets the association measure as an indicator of either the consequences or the desirability of measurement method changes, he must also recognize the inherent simplifications being relied upon. In terms of consequences, price changes *per se* are not likely to indicate fully the impact of reallocation in a regime of incomplete markets, simply because of less than complete marketability. For example, questions of a manager's nonmarketable human capital become an issue at this point, and with less than complete marketability, strict focus on market aspects may miss important dimensions of the consequences.

In terms of desirability, however, the argument is, perhaps, more subtle. Consider a strict presentation issue, as in Beaver and Dukes (1972, 1973), where the underlying depreciation and tax allocation data were available to the reader and the narrow question addressed was how to present these data. Subject to internal and external validity concerns, one might conclude that the "statement-proper" presentation yielding the highest contemporaneous association provides the data that individuals prefer to employ, and should therefore be the accountant's choice (thereby saving on users' processing costs).

But even if this line of attack is successful in pinpointing desirable (that is, efficient) modes of presentation, it falls short of answering more basic questions.[6] For example, Beaver (1972), and May and Sundem (1973), point out that this approach cannot be employed to assess the desirability of unreported alternatives such as current values (assuming that the underlying events are not reported by competing sources of information). More fundamentally (as noted by Beaver and Demski, 1974; and Gonedes and Dopuch, 1974), the approach breaks down when it is pushed beyond narrow format questions to the extreme of using market association studies to rank accounting alternatives in general. Other criticisms are summarized by Sterling and Harrison (1974, pp. 146-48).

A similar question is whether the traditional guides of market prices and the market value maximization rule can be used to rank accounting alternatives. The answer, unfortunately, is negative if the market structure is incomplete (Radner, 1974). This result is also articulated by Gonedes and Dopuch (1974). In their analysis, markets are initially assumed to be perfect and the goal of firms is to maximize the current market value of common shares; that is, firm decisions follow the market value rule. Information is regarded as merely one of the outputs that firms may produce for sale. Gonedes and Dopuch further assume that firms are capable of limiting consumption of their information output to those who actually purchase it and that no inter-user externalities arise. Under such conditions, a market for information would exist; firms could observe prices in this market and assess marginal revenue and cost relationships to determine information output. Further, share prices would reflect changes in the value of the firm associated with its information production activities. Hence market value maximization would lead to efficient resource allocation.

However, difficulties emerge if we posit that firms do *not* have the ability to limit use of produced information to those who actually purchase it. The inability to exclude nonpurchasers causes evaporation of

---

selves the results of "bad" judgments or prior beliefs and hence cannot be relied upon in the search for a "good" measurement system.

[6] Marshall (1975), for example, stresses the internal validity concerns in specifying the "abnormal performance index" as a measure of the association between unexpected earnings and unexpected price movements.

the market for information, since information can be costlessly obtained by all.[7] This induced market incompleteness precludes decisions about information production that are based on considerations of marginal revenue and cost. To illustrate, consider a firm producing information that, in the presence of an information market, would add value to the firm. However, the information produced has negative cash flow implications for the firm's noninformation activities. In the absence of an information market, share price will fall, since no increase in the firm's value due to information production will occur to offset the loss in value related to noninformation activities. Hence, as long as information markets are incomplete, no general correspondence between the desirability of information production decisions and share price movements will exist. Consequently, observation of market reactions may not be helpful in resolving certain controversies regarding accounting alternatives.

The Problem of Cost-Benefit Considerations in Accounting Theories

In assessing the desirability of various financial reporting alternatives, accounting theorists have generally not determined the benefits and costs related to their recommendations. The opinion that a specified reporting alternative, such as accounting in units of general purchasing power or extensions of interim reporting, should not be adopted because it is too costly for the benefits received is expressed frequently, but supporting data are rarely presented. This is not surprising since the benefits and costs of any proposal are exceedingly difficult to identify and measure. However, until such a demonstration occurs, it is not possible to defend conclusively a particular accounting policy against competing alternatives. More generally, except for the information economics approach that incorporates cost-benefit considerations at an abstract level, all approaches to accounting theory fail to provide explicitly for the measurement and comparison of benefits and costs of accounting options. Many accountants feel that this is a crippling weakness which will always prevent them from achieving consensus regarding solutions to accounting issues.

Thus, formally incorporating the cost-benefit orientation of information economics offers an appealing avenue of theoretical pursuit. However, difficulties exist. Most obvious is the practical issue of how one operationalizes the expected utility measures. With the proper axiomatic foundation, the mathematical existence of such measures surely is guaranteed. But this theoretical existence provides little guidance for constructing such a measure and incorporating actual numbers—as must be done to implement the approach in a real-world setting.

An even deeper problem also exists, however. That is, even the mathematical *existence* of the preference, or cost-benefit, measure may be denied in a multi-person setting. Recall that in a multiperson setting we seek nonmarket allocation criteria when considering how to intervene in or supplement a laissez faire allocation process. An example arises when the FASB considers some disclosure policy. The issue is, what criterion should govern the FASB's deliberations. And the difficulty, known as Arrow's Paradox, is that a complete and transitive ranking of the alternative criteria does not, given a set of seemingly innocuous assumptions, exist. That is, existence is denied.

Briefly, the problem as posited by Arrow (1963) is one of moving from individual to social preference. To make the problem interesting, at least two individuals and three alternatives are recognized (which is hardly a problem in an accounting setting). Arrow *imposed* four conditions that this relationship should satisfy:

1) *Universal Domain.* The individuals are unrestricted except that they must display complete and transitive preferences. Similarly, the social preference that emerges must be complete and transitive.
2) *Pareto Optimality.* If all individuals strictly prefer one choice to another,

---

[7] Similar observations emerge when we reflect on the notion of a price that "reflects" all currently available information (see Grossman and Stiglitz, 1976).

then the social ordering should strictly prefer the one to the other. This confines the choice to those alternatives that are efficient and hardly seems debatable. Abandoning it would amount to proposing a method of choice based on systematically denying those affected what they want.

3) *Independence of Irrelevant Alternatives*. If two alternative sets of individual preferences agree on a subset of the alternatives then the corresponding social preferences must agree on that subset of alternatives. This condition rules out interpersonal utility comparisons. The choice between any pair of alternatives must be based solely on the individual preferences for the two alternatives and not on any other preferences they have (such as might be used to "calibrate" interpersonal comparisons).

4) *Nondictatorship*. There does not exist an individual whose preferences are always identical to society's.

Difficulty arises because these conditions are mutually inconsistent. No such method of moving from individual to social preferences exists. As a consequence, the policy problem cannot be formulated in terms of maximizing some conceptually well-defined criterion. That is, even with a well-defined criterion for accounting system design at the individual level, we do not emerge with a specific criterion for regulation.

How, then, does one formulate the problem of regulation or policy choice? Clearly, these choices are presently made and will continue to be made. Since whatever method might be employed violates *at least* one of Arrow's conditions, one might structure the problem in terms of selecting which conditions to violate. Fundamentally, however, the criterion question is an open one.

Quite simply, then, cost-benefit analysis does not provide *the* basis for constructing a theory of accounting. Indeed, one cannot even formulate the question of guiding non-market allocations in terms of costs and benefits because, accepting Arrow's formulation of the problem, such measurements do not exist.[8]

To summarize, for some accountants, the failure to incorporate cost-benefit considerations in most theoretical approaches serves as a sufficient reason to reject those approaches. On the other hand, proper cost-benefit analysis does not appear possible with the present state of economic knowledge. This is not to say, however, that unambiguous social choice criteria cannot emerge in a multi-person setting. To the extent that the individuals involved can work out mutually acceptable side payments, any externality can be removed and Pareto-optimal solutions achieved. Nevertheless, in general cases, cost-benefit analysis cannot provide a basis for constructing an accounting theory at the present time.

Limitations of Data Expansion

In recent years a theoretical approach to external reporting issues called "data expansion" has emerged. Simply stated, proponents of this approach argue that *more information is assuredly preferable to less*. Accordingly, they suggest that many types of accounting controversies can be resolved through expanded disclosures.

Impetus for the data expansion approach arises from two distinct sources. In one view, accountants' limited knowledge of users' preferences and behavior makes it difficult to defend a single reporting option against available competing alternatives. As a consequence, it is argued that these difficult choices can be avoided by presenting more detailed disclosures or by reporting simultaneously several alternatives that satisfy some (usually unspecified) logical criteria. Sorter's "events approach" (1969) illustrates this position.

A second perspective, market efficiency, also lends support to the data expansion approach. In this view, the "efficient" market in the aggregate presumably is not misled by the form or content of accounting disclosures. As long as there

---

[8] See Beaver and Demski (1974) for an analysis of the problem in terms of the political institutions we devise to answer such questions.

are sufficient disclosures, the disclosed data will be evaluated and efficiently impounded in security prices. From the perspective of market efficiency, it makes little sense to argue over, say, which reporting format is preferable; disclosure is viewed as a means for resolving such controversies. Debates regarding alternative forms of lease accounting, for example, would constitute a trivial issue. Complete disclosure is viewed as the critical issue and where—or in what manner—the disclosure is effected is unimportant. In a similar vein, increased disclosure would be viewed by some as a means of resolving traditional measurement controversies. Reporting historical and current-cost numbers to market participants, for example, eliminates the controversy over inflation accounting.

The net result of both views is the same. There has emerged a theoretical position centering around increased disclosure in lieu of resolution of issues by reliance on traditional theoretical analysis. But the appeal of data expansion has been resisted on three grounds: (1) physiological considerations, (2) cognitive processing limitations, and (3) economic efficiency.

The most obvious criticism of data expansion is physiological. Beyond some point, additional data could overwhelm a decision maker and make it physically impossible for him to consider and impound incremental messages—the familiar "information overload" problem. Of course, this criticism does not apply when the incremental data are of modest proportions and the user is not inundated with data.

However, even when the proposed data expansion is small, an important psychological effect suggests that even modest increases in disclosure are not "costless." Increased disclosure levels increase the *perceived* complexity of the environment. Abundant psychological testing evidence indicates that such changes in perceived environmental complexity induce changes in decision makers' cognitive processing capabilities (e.g., Schroder, Driver, and Streufert, 1967). These cognitive processing changes, in turn, can decrease the effectiveness of decision making by causing decision makers to revert to a more concrete conceptual level in an attempt to cope with the new, more complex environment (Driver and Streufert, 1969).

The relevance of the cognitive processing effect to accounting reporting issues was initially raised at a theoretical level (Revsine, 1970b, 1970c, 1973). Subsequent empirical tests in an accounting setting explored the potentially adverse effects of increasing environmental complexity on various kinds of decision styles (Driver and Mock, 1975). Dermer (1973) also examined the effect of personality variables on this process. From a psychological perspective, results of preliminary research indicate that data expansion is not a panacea. Beyond a certain point, even relatively modest increases in reported data raise the possibility of adverse decision-making effects.[9]

The desirability of a data expansion approach to external reporting is also unclear when the issue is examined from the traditional perspective of the economic consequences of information. Here two deep concerns arise, even if we assume that the reporting alternatives are costless. First, placement—as long as the disclosure is made—may not be a totally neutral aspect of the problem. With alternative placement options, choice of one as opposed to another may "signal" some additional economic aspect. For example, footnote versus statement-proper disclosure of a potential liability from pending litigation may "signal" different management beliefs as to the likelihood that the litigation will be adverse. Similarly, the manner in which forecasts are presented may convey informa-

---

[9] This brief summary necessarily omits certain issues. For example, are information specialists subject to similar adverse effects of increasing complexity? What little evidence is available suggests that the adverse decision effect arises among both abstract and concrete decision makers (Streufert and Schroder, 1965; Driver and Streufert, 1969; and Streufert, 1970). However, the issues of personality variables (Dermer, 1973) and decision style (Driver and Mock, 1975) have also been explored to determine the generalizability of these findings. Furthermore, over time the level of complexity that leads to adverse effects may be increased as learning takes place (Miller and Gordon, 1975). However, the general point remains: the possibility of adverse decision effects cannot be ignored in data expansion proposals.

tion about the quality of the forecasts. This type of signalling effect is discussed by Spence (1973) and Stiglitz (1975).[10]

Second, disclosing or producing "more" information even if it is costless may not be beneficial. In fact, it may be strictly harmful. In a multi-person setting, such as that of numerous users of accounting reports, it does not necessarily follow that *public* information is a superior good. Some may be harmed by production of such information, even if it is costless (see Ho and Chu, 1974; Baiman, 1975; and Demski and Feltham, 1976). Perhaps more significantly, in a recently published paper, Hart (1975) demonstrates that in a regime of incomplete markets, opening new markets, say, by providing additional accounting measures on which to make event-contingent trades, may not be an economically defensible act. More information, in other words, even if free, need not be beneficial in a multi-person setting.

In summary, the basic tenet of the data expansion approach—more information is assuredly preferable to less—does not apply in either a general economic setting or from a cognitive information processing perspective. Accordingly, theories that rely on data expansion have not achieved widespread acceptance.

Summary

In this chapter, we have reviewed a variety of reasons why individual accountants may be dissatisfied with the various approaches to developing an accounting theory. We have not attempted to provide an exhaustive enumeration; instead, our discussion illustrates major issues. Although the reader may well have additional points of contention or criticism, this limited discussion should suggest the breadth of the problem.

We urge the reader to avoid reading any partisan intent into our use of the words "criticisms" and "points of contention." We are *not* assessing specific formulations of accounting theories. Nor are we defending or criticizing any particular theoretical approach. Rather, we have attempted to propound reasons why none of the available theoretical approaches has yielded a *sufficient and compelling basis* for specifying the content of external financial reports. That is, we have examined several detailed points of conflict which collectively explain why no theoretical approach has achieved consensus acceptance.

---

[10] Further note that a firm may have elected to have its statements audited before specific requirements were imposed simply because such behavior was a signal of the quality of the statements and the integrity of the management.

Chapter 4

Difficulties in Achieving Consensus: A General View

Accounting researchers, academic committees, and professionally sponsored policy groups have attempted, over the years, to formulate theories of accounting. In Chapter 3, we acknowledged a prevailing expectation among accountants that those efforts would lead to some sort of unified theory that would provide a sufficient and compelling basis for specifying the content of external financial reports. We then summarized a number of problems that may have prevented any of the available theoretical approaches from rising to a position of prominence relative to the others.

Yet, even if each separate approach is perceived to contain serious flaws, members of the accounting community might still expect that a process of argument and counterargument would eventually promote theoretical closure. That is, many might consider the process of theoretical development in accounting to be a type of evolution. If that be the case, we need only to continue the collective struggle to adapt and modify our theoretical structures as environmental changes occur.

From an evolutionary perspective, however, specific formulations of accounting theory will continually face the prospect of diminishing relevance unless piecemeal modifications are undertaken to adapt the theory formulation to environmental changes. Furthermore, if environmental changes are frequent, the existing theoretical structure is bound to be under constant pressure; that is, the implications of the theory may not be judged as compelling reasons to constrain or specify the content of external reports.

The evolutionary view of accounting theory formation has considerable appeal. It obviously allows for the existence of important, unresolved issues. Furthermore, it also holds the optimistic promise of movement toward resolution of these issues.

In spite of these features, the committee is led to consider an alternative view. Our reason is that the accounting literature of the past decade or two appears inconsistent with the evolutionary view of accounting theory development. Consider these examples: (1) the apparent consensus on the "matching and attaching" approach to theory formation is disintegrating; (2) issues that are either irrelevant or unresolvable under that approach continue to be recycled; and (3) there is an expanded array of alternative approaches to theory formation, none of which looms as an apparent successor to the cost-based approach of matching and attaching. All these factors suggest that changes in the process of theorizing in accounting may be more revolutionary than evolutionary. Such a perspective was developed as a general view of science by Thomas S. Kuhn (1970).[1]

Achieving Paradigm Acceptance

In his treatise on the pattern of changes in scientific thought, Kuhn introduces the concept of "paradigms," which he contextually defines as conceptual and instrumental frameworks that "provide models from which spring particular coherent tra-

---

[1] We are sensitive to the potential validity of criticisms that analyses (such as Kuhn's) of scientific practices and methodologies probably were not intended to apply and, in fact, may not be applicable to such diverse areas of intellectual activity as physical sciences, social sciences, and accounting. For example, we note Mark Blaug's conclusion that "both Kuhn and Lakatos jeer at modern psychology and sociology as pre-paradigmatic, proto-sciences, and although economics seems to be exempted from the charge, Lakatos seems to think that even economists have never seriously committed themselves to the principle of falsifiability" (1976). No doubt the vast bulk of accountants' work falls victim to the charge levied upon psychologists, sociologists, and economists. Thus, we must recognize the possibility that Kuhn's views on the development of science may apply less forcefully to accounting than would be appropriate for other areas of intellectual endeavor which have richer scientific traditions. Nevertheless, we note striking similarities in the general objectives of science and accounting, and our search for rationales that apply to the existing stage of accounting thought suggests significant insights to be gained from the comparisons drawn in this chapter.

ditions of scientific research" (p. 10). The paradigm of an individual scientist specifies the kinds of problems he perceives to be interesting. It circumscribes the empirical domain over which the individual's theories and research are applied. It indicates the kinds of tests or standards that are used to adjudicate contradictory theoretical propositions. And, after a time of research and theorizing, if a paradigm is shared by the scientific community, it leads the research and theorizing processes to a single, prevailing theory of the area. In other words, a paradigm constitutes a kind of world view and focus for research. Kuhn observes that "men whose research is based on shared paradigms are committed to the same rules and standards for scientific practice" (p. 11).

The current accounting scene includes a wide diversity of issues that are deemed to be important by individual researchers; it also includes a wide diversity of research methods employed to address these issues. Such diversity is pervasive. Some authors, for example, consider the issues raised by others to be trivial and undeserving of attention. Similarly, debate on the relative merits and weaknesses of alternative research methods provokes a constant stream of argumentative articles, symposia, and speeches. In terms of Kuhn's description, this state of affairs would suggest that accounting theorists do not have a shared paradigm. Rather, we tend to have different perspectives of the world, perceive different issues to be of significance, appeal to different sets of empirical phenomena in searching for answers to these issues, and accept different tests or standards for resolving these issues. Further, if one subscribes to the Kuhnian view, it is highly unlikely that consensus on these matters will occur by a cumulative process of scientific inquiry.[2]

---

[2] We would emphasize the intention of this chapter to bring additional perspective to the array of theoretical conflict in accounting; the chapter presents one possible view of the factors that collectively represent a lack of clear direction and focus within the community of accounting theorists and researchers. Readers should not infer a committee decision to reject alternative perspectives, such as might be provided by Imre Lakatos. Indeed, Blaug's (1976) thoughtful comparison

Contrary to the idea that scientific knowledge progresses in a cumulative, evolutionary pattern, Kuhn offers a revolutionary description of scientific progress, which proceeds in the following order:
1. acceptance of a paradigm;
2. working within that paradigm by doing "normal" science;
3. becoming dissatisfied with that paradigm;
4. searching for a new paradigm;
5. accepting a new paradigm.

The most difficult thing to explain is the reason scientists collectively accept a new paradigm. It seems clear that the reason

---

of Kuhn's and Lakatos' alternative views on the history of scientific thought is recommended for assistance in assessing the significance of Kuhn's arguments, as well as for suggesting some of the potential shortcomings inherent in the present application of Kuhn's work. See also Lakatos and Musgrave (1970).

In addition, this chapter is not intended to infer that the existing state of theoretical conflict in accounting must necessarily be understood in terms of a philosophical perspective of the history of science. Other plausible views are possible. One example of an alternative view arises from an economic interpretation, whereby we (1) assume rational behavior, (2) recognize sufficient externalities to yield some kind of central policy making as an efficient means of establishing accounting practices, and then (3) perceive the alternative approaches to developing accounting theories not as "paradigms" or as "scientific theories" but rather as individual or group proposals for specifying how accounting ought to be done, or specifying how accountants ought to go about deciding how accounting will be done. In this situation, we observe that the problem of selecting the best accounting policies cannot be set up in a cost-benefit setting because the requisite concept of social preference is missing (a la Arrow's theorem). Also, whatever policies will finally be chosen will depend upon the institution or structure by which the policies are chosen. Even if the decision is to select the policies by voting, the outcome will depend upon the voting system we impose.

From this economic perspective, disagreement ensues because we have heterogeneous opinions and tastes, and there is no neat, defensible method of putting our conflicting tastes and beliefs into a grand social function. Thus, the problem is by nature one of confrontation, and there is no generally accepted way of coming to agreement. Different "theories" or proposals lead to different resource allocations, and we generally have conflicting views over which resource allocations are better, and there is no theory to guide us in counterbalancing conflicting opinions. So it is understandable that the current state of "theoretical" conflict in accounting exists and does not appear to be resolvable at the present time.

they reject an existing paradigm is because anomalies arise, which cause scientists to become dissatisfied with that paradigm. This dissatisfaction motivates a subset of the scientists to search for a new paradigm while other scientists continue to try to work within the older paradigm and to either rationalize or ignore the anomalies.

What is happening in accounting today can be described in similar terms. There are a number of theorists who have become dissatisfied with the old matching-attaching approach to specifying the content of financial reports. In its place, they have turned to several alternative approaches to answering accounting questions. Depending upon the level of generalization at which one might choose to apply this view, the decision-usefulness approach and the economic approach to analyzing accounting information issues might each be treated as an alternative paradigm. At another level, one might treat each of the alternative valuation schemes as reflecting alternative approaches to resolving accounting questions.

Not all of these alternative paradigms are necessarily advanced as a sufficient basis for making accounting policy decisions; often proponents of a particular approach readily acknowledge numerous uncertainties and unsettled implementation issues. Indeed, some proponents of an alternative may caution against the suggestion that the alternative constitutes an approach to theory formation in accounting at all. In these cases it would appear that an alternative is intended only to bring interesting evidence to bear upon the matter of making policy decisions. Nevertheless, each of the accounting approaches currently advocated involves a unique way of looking at the accounting problem at hand, whatever it may happen to be. Indeed, each approach tends to self-select the problems with which it will deal as well as the means it will employ to attack these problems. In short, each approach begins to take on the attributes of a distinctive paradigm. At the same time that many theorists and researchers are working out the accounting implications of these new paradigms, others are unwilling to accept any of the new paradigms. Rather they continue to try to solve problems within the context of the old paradigms.

In this state of dissatisfaction with existing paradigms we can note that each theorist attempts to provide his own foundation for the field. In regard to Newton's theory of optics, Kuhn writes:

> Being able to take no common body of belief for granted, each writer on physical optics felt forced to build his field anew from its foundations. In doing so, his choice of supporting observation and experiment was relatively free, for there was no standard set of methods or of phenomena that every optical writer felt forced to employ and explain. Under these circumstances, the dialogue of the resulting books was often directed as much to the members of other schools as it was to nature. That pattern is not unfamiliar in a number of creative fields today, nor is it incompatible with significant discovery and invention. (p. 13)

This seems to be an apt description of what is happening in accounting at the present time. Many theorists seem to feel the need to start from some basic foundations to build the field of accounting anew. For example, a recent managerial accounting study started with very fundamental kinds of observations and then attempted to reconstruct the discipline on the basis of those foundations (Demski and Feltham, 1976). Theorizing from efficient markets research has proceeded in a similar vein (Fama, 1970). Valuation theorists have also started with very elemental or fundamental assumptions. For example, Chambers drew heavily on a large number of other disciplines in order to derive his particular theory of valuation (1966).

One of the few attitudes that is shared by most contemporary accounting theorists is dissatisfaction with the prevailing matching-attaching paradigm. They share little else in regard to problems that ought to be solved or methods that ought to be employed. Indeed, different individuals may not even agree on what constitutes a "fact" in the absence of a shared paradigm (Sterling, 1970b). Therefore, since different theorists may each employ different implicit paradigms, they may simultaneously each perceive different facts. As

Kuhn makes clear, this is not unique to accounting:

> Excluding those fields, like mathematics and astronomy, in which the first firm paradigms date from prehistory and also those, like biochemistry, that arose by division and recombination of specialties already matured, the situations outlined above are historically typical.... In parts of biology—the study of heredity, for example—the first universally received paradigms are still more recent; and it remains an open question what parts of social sciences have yet acquired such paradigms at all. History suggests that the road to a firm research consensus is extraordinarily arduous. (p. 15)

Obviously, the road to a research consensus in accounting has been extraordinarily arduous as is evidenced by the fact that we have not achieved that consensus. Kuhn continues:

> History also suggests, however, some reasons for the difficulties encountered on that road. In the absence of a paradigm or some candidate for paradigm, all of the facts that could possibly pertain to the development of a given science are likely to seem equally relevant. As a result, early fact-gathering is a far more nearly random activity than the one that subsequent scientific development makes. (p. 15)

Thus, in the absence of an agreed-upon paradigm, there is no consensus regarding which environmental characteristics are especially important as a basis for theory development. All facts appear to be equally relevant. Some theorists will then suggest a particular paradigm which, among other things, specifies what are facts and what are nonfacts. *The problem is that one paradigm will likely specify a different set of facts from that specified by a competing paradigm.*

This is the process that results in disjoint paradigms and, in turn, is the reason that one paradigm cannot be used to judge or assess another. Kuhn states it directly:

> We have already seen several reasons why the proponents of competing paradigms must fail to make complete contact with each other's viewpoints. Collectively these reasons have been described as the incommensurability of the pre- and postrevolutionary normal-scientific traditions, and we need only recapitulate them briefly here. In the first place, the proponents of competing paradigms will often disagree about the lists of problems that any candidate for paradigm must resolve. (p. 148)

He goes on to point out that:

> Communication across the revolutionary divide [of different paradigms] is inevitably partial. (p. 149)

The proponents of competing paradigms almost inevitably find their argumentative discourse to be fraught with communication failures. That is, those who employ different paradigms find it difficult to communicate with one another. Numerous examples can be observed in accounting debates. Consider a discussion of accounting for special purpose manufacturing equipment that has no resale value, where the paradigm of one discussant has led him to adopt a current exit price theory of accounting valuation and the paradigm of the other discussant has led him to adopt a replacement cost theory of accounting valuation. In proposing the balance sheet amount to be reported, the two discussants would likely disagree. Further, in attempting to resolve the dispute, the two discussants would likely appeal to different facts. The exit price accountant would look to the zero resale value of the equipment, while the current entry price accountant would generally look to the replacement cost of the equipment. In the usual case, the exit price would be an irrelevant fact to the entry price accountant, and to the exit price accountant the entry price would usually be irrelevant to the investigation. Thus, the divergent paradigms employed by each party lead to different perceptions of what "facts" should be observed to resolve the problem. After a while, each party to the discussion may conclude that the other simply doesn't understand the problem, or doesn't understand the role of accounting. What one sees as relevant "facts," the other may reject as totally irrelevant to the situation.

Kuhn continues with:

> ... the third and most fundamental as-

pect of the incommensurability of competing paradigms. In a sense that I am unable to explicate further, the proponents of competing paradigms practice their trades in different worlds.... Both are looking at the world, and what they look at has not changed but in some areas they see different things, and they see them in different relations one to the other. That is why a law that cannot even be demonstrated to one group of scientists may occasionally seem intuitively obvious to another. (p 150)

This type of disagreement is evident in accounting also. Some things that appear to be too obvious to require explicit statement by one group are seen by another group as unfounded assertions that are unacceptable unless supported by evidence and/or deductive reasoning. Kuhn argues, however, that these different views cannot be reconciled by either logic or empirics. Instead, they are revolutionary shifts in world views:

Just because it is a transition between incommensurables, the transition between competing paradigms cannot be made a step at a time, forced by logic and neutral experience. Like the gestalt switch, it must occur all at once (though not necessarily in an instant) or not at all. (p. 150)

Thus, paradigm acceptance is like a gestalt switch, a change in world views. That is, it is not possible to prove that one paradigm is superior to another; instead a scientist either sees the new paradigm or he does not. Butterfield (1957) summarized the point in describing a switch from one paradigm to another in the physical sciences. He said that the change was not in the facts observed, but instead it was "a transposition in the minds of the scientists" (p. 17).

Just as Kuhn could not explicate what precise factors finally precipitate general acceptance of a specific paradigm, this committee is unable to identify the factors that would lead to such a consensus in accounting. It may be another instance of the "aha" phenomenon. That is, some scientists may look at a paradigm, make a gestalt switch, and, in effect, say, "Aha, I understand that better now." It is a psychological question of great magnitude. For example, the paradigm of some accounting theorists results in an information economics approach to analyzing accounting issues, which is accepted perhaps because the theorists believe that it offers great promise for the resolution of accounting problems. Other theorists have not made this particular gestalt switch and resist the information economics paradigm. They accept other, equally defensible paradigms (such as the decision model approach) and believe that their paradigms offer more promise for resolving accounting issues. The phenomenon is apparently psychological, as suggested by the fact that some of our greatest scientists have continued to resist particular paradigms even after they had become well accepted by the majority of the scientific community. Even if the accounting community eventually develops a consensus on a single paradigm, we will not be able to criticize those that were discarded:

Still more men, convinced of the new view's fruitfulness, will adopt the new mode of practicing normal science, until at last only a few elderly holdouts remain. And even they, we cannot say, are wrong. (Kuhn, p. 159)

The revolutionary perspective of science is applied to accounting as a plausible means of interpreting the current condition of accounting theory. There are a number of people offering different paradigms. A few have been converted to each of the paradigms but there is no consensus at the present time. Furthermore, it would appear as though there is no quick way to achieve a consensus among competing paradigms. Exhaustive research efforts, fiat pronouncements, and exhortations will not necessarily work. Perhaps one day soon all others will say "aha" and accept one of the competing paradigms and begin to do the puzzle-solving and mopping-up operations of normal science. Note, however, that this is a description of the process, not an explanation. Scientists must admit that at present the process of paradigm selection is not well understood. The process can be described, but describing it does not assist us in the actual selection of a particular paradigm.

Empirical and Logical Testing of Competing Paradigms

The traditional scientific response to a problem of competing alternatives is to examine the logical consistency and empirical implications of each alternative. Competing paradigms should lead to competing theories. Following the logical positivist tradition, the prerequisite criteria for acceptance of a theory are that it be logically consistent and empirically supportable.[3] If these criteria can be applied to select between competing theories, perhaps they can also serve, by inference, to select between the competing paradigms from which the respective theories were derived.

There are, however, fundamental flaws in this approach, some of which are rather technical. One easily understandable flaw is that all theories are incomplete, in the sense that additional research is always required. The research process in science is one of continuing to make logical connections or empirical tests. Thus, no theory can pass those two tests completely, because the testing processes themselves are never complete. Even within the context of a single paradigm, therefore, the testing of competing propositions and theories may not provide a permanent basis for selection between the alternatives.

A second, and more damaging, flaw in the approach of using logical and empirical tests to select between competing theories becomes apparent if the competing theories issue from competing paradigms. Kuhn explains the problem in the context of discussing the reasons for chemists' acceptance of Dalton's paradigm:

> ... it is hard to make nature fit a paradigm. That is why the puzzles of normal science are so challenging and also why measurements undertaken without a paradigm so seldom lead to any conclusions at all. Chemists could not, therefore, simply accept Dalton's theory on the evidence, for much of that was still negative. Instead, even after accepting the theory, they had still to beat nature into line, a process which, in the event, took almost another generation. When it was done, even the percentage composition of well-known compounds was different. The data themselves had changed. (p. 135)

Thus, at the time a theory is proposed, it may not pass the typical empirical tests; the evidence may still be negative. Instead of subjecting the theory to empirical tests, researchers may have to "beat nature into line" by developing new tests within the context of the new paradigm. The acceptance of Dalton's paradigm involved a gestalt switch that changed the very perceptions of the scientists who were doing the research. It is this new world view which allows the scientists to change the data. And these new, changed data are necessary if the new theory is to pass the empirical tests. A recent illustration of this process is the testing of the accounting implications of efficient securities markets. In order to assess the information content and disclosure implications of that theory, analytic devices such as the API metric and other tests related to the capital asset pricing model had to be developed. Without these devices, the theory's implications for accounting were untestable. Thus, there must be at least some threshold acceptance of a new paradigm before tests of the theory arising from the paradigm are possible.

The point is that, although theories must pass tests of logical consistency and empirical predictability, one cannot expect these tests to provide a conclusive basis for selecting from among competing paradigms. Ultimately, the design of the tests as well as the perception of the data to which they apply are dependent upon, or defined in terms of, the paradigm that is to be tested. Logic and empirics do not, therefore, provide a sufficient basis for selecting between competing paradigms.

Judgmental Selection of a Paradigm

Although scientists cannot explain the precise reasons for the acceptance of different paradigms, it is possible to describe certain types of differences among paradigms. One set of such differences relates to the paradigms' empirical domains.

---

[3] Other criteria such as simplicity and elegance could be introduced but these are clearly subordinate to logical and empirical testability.

Each of the currently competing accounting paradigms tends to specify a different empirical domain over which an accounting theory ought to apply.

For example, one paradigm, which could be labeled the "anthropological approach," specifies the professional practices of accountants as the empirical domain of accounting. Following this paradigm, accounting theory is formulated as a rationalization of, and by drawing inferences from, extant accounting practices. Another paradigm rests largely upon the behavior of stock markets to provide the empirical domain over which accounting theory is constructed and applied. Still another general view of accounting specifies the decision processes of individuals and/or extant decision theories as the empirical domain of accounting theory.[4] This tripartite categorization can be further expanded to incorporate both the ideal income approach and the information economics approach, each of which suggests a somewhat unique empirical domain of accounting. It was precisely these differences in empirical domain that provided the organizational format of Chapters 1 and 2.

As we have already suggested, the differences in empirical domain that pervade each paradigm reflect basic differences in world views. Each paradigm has different embedded premises and objectives; accordingly, each rather naturally focuses on precisely those empirical phenomena that are highlighted by those premises and are relevant or controllable in achieving the desired outcomes. When viewed from this perspective, it is apparent that no view can be *per se* "correct" or "incorrect." Instead, each must be evaluated in conjunction with contextual factors and personal preferences.

Because the choice among paradigms from this perspective must necessarily be judgmental, proponents of different paradigms frequently make basic value judgments (either explicit or implicit) and then argue that their paradigm, on the basis of those value judgments, is superior to competing ones. Kuhn argues that this is the usual procedure in science:

> Like the choice between competing political institutions, that between competing paradigms proves to be a choice between incompatible modes of community life. Because it has that character, the choice is not and cannot be determined merely by the evaluative procedures characteristic of normal science, for these depend in part upon a particular paradigm, and that paradigm is at issue. When paradigms enter, as they must, into a debate about paradigm choice, their role is necessarily circular. Each group uses its own paradigm to argue in that paradigm's defense.
>
> The resulting circularity does not, of course, make the arguments wrong or even ineffectual. The man who premises a paradigm when arguing in its defense can nonetheless provide a clear exhibit of what scientific practice will be like for those who adopt the new view of nature. That exhibit can be immensely persuasive, often compellingly so. Yet, whatever its force, the status of the circular argument is only that of persuasion. It cannot be made logically or even probabilistically compelling for those who refuse to step into the circle. (p. 94)

The lengthy debate over alternative accounting theories obviously has not led to closure. Perhaps the extent to which each theory's proponents employ circular arguments is most easily discerned by those who are aligned with the alternative theories. Kuhn concludes that such circular arguments are inevitable, but not necessarily ineffectual. Individuals can sometimes be persuaded by this kind of debate. Nevertheless, we should not expect that the continued debate over accounting theories will naturally lead to a dominant consensus.[5] Note that we are not in any sense calling for a moratorium on this kind of debate. Rather, we are attempting to articu-

---

[4] For an elaboration of this classification of paradigms by empirical domain, see Sterling (1970b, pp. 449-54).

[5] For a somewhat different view on this point, see Wells (1976). That article, which parallels our discussion at several points, did not come to our attention until this document was completed.

late realistic expectations about the consequences of this activity.

Summary

The purpose of this chapter has been to develop a plausible explanation for the lack of progress in achieving accounting theory consensus. An expanding array of accounting theories and/or theoretical approaches suggests the existence of several competing paradigms. Each paradigm implicitly incorporates individual beliefs and premises that cannot be proved or disproved in a logical sense. Further, the "facts" towards which a theory is directed are themselves a function of the paradigm embraced by the observer. Thus, rigorous experimental testing, while valuable in the sense of influencing long-run psychological sets, cannot be used to resolve the problem of selecting a single paradigm for accounting. As a consequence, defenders of a particular paradigm are forced to rely on persuasion rather than logic and empirics in attempting to defend a proposal. While consensus may eventually develop, the transformation that occurs is primarily a psychological matter rather than a dispassionately intellectual phenomenon.

Chapter 5

Implications

A committee such as this is formed periodically in order to assess the state of development of accounting theory. Ours was not a research assignment; committees cannot efficiently conduct research. Instead, our role was to survey the accounting theory literature. The benefits of this process may be twofold. First, by its very nature, a survey requires generalization and thus emphasizes important, dominant themes. This focus eliminates irrelevancies and makes primary messages more distinct. Highlighting important points that are obscured by the sheer complexity of the unclassified environment often generates new perspectives and insights, as well. Second, a survey may also clarify and underscore issues that were not explicit in the original sources. Different language or a more dispassionate, neutral perspective is frequently helpful in interpreting and broadly disseminating somewhat esoteric—and hence potentially obscure—research findings. We hope that this report accomplishes these two objectives and thereby provides a useful perspective regarding accounting theory approaches.

Implications For Research

In addition to these objectives, committee statements of this genre might be expected to have an impact on future researchers and research activities. In this domain three major "messages" emerge for researchers in accounting and for those who utilize the output of such research.

Perhaps the most fundamental implication of this document is that statements and pronouncements by "authoritative" bodies—even those comprised of accounting theorists—cannot themselves be expected to lead to near-term closure in the theory area. Our reason for emphasizing this point is that it is in marked contrast with the sentiment that apparently prevails in the accounting community. Many have looked with anticipation to past statements of accounting objectives and theory reports as a means for resolving theoretical debates. Once the awaited report appears, however, there is usually disappointment when it becomes apparent that the document does not receive immediate acceptance and thus does not lead to a cessation of debate. Some might then deem the report to be a "failure." This committee statement will, it is hoped, put the issue of theory closure into proper perspective and thereby reduce unrealistic expectations. Our message is clear: *theory closure cannot be dictated*. Even if based upon rigorous analysis, theories are inevitably derived from the experiential "sets" of those proposing them. Such sets (or paradigms) utilized in viewing the world cannot be regarded as uniquely correct. Many divergent sets may simultaneously possess inherent "truth" content. The eventual acceptance of one such approach arises from its explanatory power or ability to resolve anomalies. In other words, a theory achieves such dominant acceptance because of its demonstrated efficacy over time, not because of its espousal by some group (for example, of nine academics) that subjectively deems it to be superior.

A second basic message of this document is that *external reporting theory has a wider scope than that which has been generally perceived*. In the past, the theory realm has been thought to be limited to basic measurement controversies, nature of users' information desires, cognitive processing characteristics, and other similar issues. The institutional framework by which the policy-making process is accomplished has usually been taken as given. However, this committee report emphasizes that the institutional structure and procedures by which this structure operates are *themselves* a part of external reporting theory. This perspective immediately introduces questions regarding the desirability of regulatory intervention and the form such intervention should take, if needed. At present, studies of the socio-political process as it relates to accounting policy information, voting strategies, means for eliciting "true" preferences, and similar issues have not been widely applied to external reporting issues. However, as discussed in our report, these too are a legitimate, albeit neglected, element of external reporting theory deserving of research attention.

Finally, this report has isolated areas of disagreement between theory proposals. Explicitly recognizing basic differences between theories could lead to at least two potential benefits in future research. First, it could serve to reduce the endless argumentation regarding imperfectly understood or even hidden assumptions and consequences that currently inhibits theory progress. Second, recognizing inherent differences among theories could place in bold relief the nature of the private and social welfare tradeoffs that may have to be made in choosing among policy alternatives.

To illustrate this more concretely, consider the following example. At present, one of the most prevalent theoretical approaches employed in contemporary research is the decision-model approach. In its standard form, this approach explores means for providing relevant information to a designated user group. Accordingly, the analytic focus is limited to that group and explores only the expected consequences of the information for their decision effectiveness. But it was indicated in Chapter 3 that this approach ignores the potential economic impact of the theory proposal on other users and even nonusers of financial information. In other words, the decision-model analysis is a partial equilibrium approach. This raises the possibility of objections to such proposals on several bases. Notwithstanding the benefits accruing to the user group that formed the basis for the analysis, some may object to a decision model proposal because of unfavorable repercussions to other societal segments; that is, the issue may be one of distributive welfare. Similarly, the social costs incurred in generating "better" information to the selected group may not be commensurate with the benefits expected to accrue to society. Frequently, the real issues underlying debates of this sort are not recognized. Irresolvable arguments ensue because the "benefits" perceived by proponents of a proposal may be irrelevant or inconsequential to its critics.

Prior to this committee report, partialities of this sort may not have been widely recognized as inherent in various theory approaches. By delineating these scope limitations, needless argumentation may be avoided. How might this take place? We hope that this will follow from general acceptance of the view adopted herein regarding accounting theory. Thus, our third basic message is that *all theory approaches are flawed when viewed from the perspective of some alternative approach*. This problem cannot be avoided. Hence, it is useless to seek the "universally appropriate" theory approach. At best, one approach can take cognizance of its own limitations and attempt to address omitted issues that are likely to generate disagreement when the results are viewed from the perspective of some alternative theory approach.

Summarizing, one of the primary objectives of this committee document is to promote a deeper understanding of the nature of accounting theories, how they differ, and the issues that arise in selecting among the various alternatives. We concluded that theory choices are vitally dependent upon the experiential set and preferences of the observer. Consequently, rigorous analytic techniques serve only a limited role in this area as an initial screening device, that is, as a means for identifying and eliminating proposals that are logically inconsistent or erroneous. Proposals that survive this analytic screen must gain acceptance on some other basis—their explanatory or predictive power, ability to resolve existing anomalies, or conformity to prevailing social preferences. Clearly, research plays an important role in this post-screening choice process too. However, dispassionate logical analysis is only a necessary, not a sufficient, condition for eventual theory acceptance. Seemingly, the crucial role of the sufficient conditions has not been widely understood in the past. But failure to comprehend this element of the theory choice process leads to attempts to impose such closure by a process that might be termed "theoretical fiat." Such efforts have historically been largely unproductive. Our belief is that a better understanding of the nature of the total theory acceptance process will reduce expectations for achieving theory closure by fiat and redirect researchers to more promising avenues. Thus, the approach used in this committee document was selected with the expectation that it will facilitate such research progress. It is to be hoped that this expectation will be fulfilled.

Implications For Policy

When considering issues of immediate and crucial importance, policy makers do not have the luxury of sidestepping difficult, unresolved questions. Life goes on, decisions must be made, and policy choices occur. Recognizing these facts, our committee statement has certain implications for policy makers seeking direction from accounting theories.

The central message to policy makers is that *until consensus paradigm acceptance occurs, the utility of accounting theories in aiding policy decisions is partial*. Competing theories merely provide a basis for forming opinions on what must remain inherently subjective judgments. While it is true that consensus will frequently develop on certain points, usually this consensus only narrows the range of disagreement; it often does not resolve the basic issue that gives rise to the underlying problem. That is, consensus about peripheral improvements may occasionally emanate from applying a theory, but the basic underlying choice issues continue to be disputatious.

A non-accounting example illustrates this point. Consider the issue of whether or not capital punishment is justified on a social welfare basis. At this level, numerous theories abound. Most are inconsistent with one another and it is impossible to *objectively* state that one such theory dominates all others. Hence the issue of capital punishment is unresolvable by theoretical debate alone. On this issue, social action is dependent upon the *subjective* beliefs and preferences of policy makers. Various theories may be instrumental in shaping the beliefs of individual policy makers, but no basis for *objectively* demonstrating the superiority of any one theory exists.

Notwithstanding the continuing disagreement on the overriding basic issue, certain subordinated issues relating to capital punishment are virtually unanimously agreed upon. That is, we are often able to conclude that a particular change was for the general good. Take, for example, the change from processing executions by drawing and quartering the criminal to execution by guillotine, hanging, electric chair, or any of the more modern forms of execution. The distributive and aggregative welfare effects of these changes defy rigorous analysis. Yet, we would expect general consensus that this was an example of improvement in professional practice.

In a similar vein, virtually all external reporting issues involve social welfare trade-offs. Depending on the particular topic, theories may occasionally narrow the range of choice by indicating a dominant consensus regarding some facet of the basic issue. Forms of execution is a non-accounting illustration; the policy change which long ago included income statements in published financial reports is an example from an accounting setting. Frequently, accounting theories will also be useful to policy makers by providing an improved basis for reaching what must now be considered to be an essentially subjective judgment. That is, theories may be helpful insofar as they apprise policy makers of the underlying issues and clarify the trade-offs implicit in various approaches. But in the absence of paradigm acceptance, it is unrealistic to expect accounting theory to provide unequivocal policy guidance. Different theories will point to different policies. These theories arise from different paradigms. Since there is no rigorous analytic means for choosing between paradigms, there is similarly no rigorous means for choosing between theories or their derivative policy implications.

This limited theory role will not necessarily persist in the long run, nor is it unique to accounting.[1] Changes will occur

---

[1] As an analogy, consider the equivocal guidance that competing economic theories provide to economic policy makers.

if, and when, consensus regarding an accounting paradigm is once again achieved. Until such time, however, expectations about the role of theory in guiding policy must be realistic. In clarifying the role of theory, one of our objectives is to indicate the futility of attempting to dictate "ultimate theoretical truths." This theory consensus may or may not be achieved in the near term. If it is achieved, it will arise because of continued accounting theory research and debate about the product of such research. However, the crucial point is that theory consensus cannot be imposed, not by this group nor by any other. Whatever future influence theory has on policy making will be achieved by continued argumentation, new theory development, and debate, not by fiat.

Bibliography

Abdel-khalik, A. R. (1971). "User Preference Ordering Value: A Model." *The Accounting Review* 46 (July, 1971) 457-71.

Akerlof, G. (1970). "The Market for 'Lemons': Quality Uncertainty and the Market Mechanism." *The Quarterly Journal of Economics* 84 (August, 1970) 488-500.

Alexander, S. S. (1950). "Income Measurement in a Dynamic Economy." *Five Monographs on Business Income.* New York: The Study Group on Business Income, The American Institute of (Certified Public) Accountants, 1950. Also see: Alexander, S. S., "Income Measurement in a Dynamic Economy" Revised by D. Solomons. *Studies in Accounting Theory.* W. T. Baxter and S. Davidson, eds. Homewood, Ill.: Richard D. Irwin, Inc., 1962.

American Accounting Association (1936). Executive Committee. "Accounting Principles Underlying Corporate Financial Statements." *The Accounting Review* 11 (June, 1936) 187-91.

American Accounting Association (1941). Executive Committee. "Accounting Principles Underlying Corporate Financial Statements." *The Accounting Review* 16 (June, 1941) 133-9.

American Accounting Association (1955). Committee on Concepts and Standards Underlying Corporate Financial Statements. "Standards of Disclosure for Published Financial Reports." Supplementary Statement No. 8. *The Accounting Review* 30 (July, 1955) 400-4.

American Accounting Association (1957). Committee on Concepts and Standards Underlying Corporate Financial Statements. "Accounting and Reporting Standards for Corporate Financial Statements, 1957 Revision." *The Accounting Review* 32 (October, 1957) 536-546.

American Accounting Association (1966). Committee to Prepare a Statement of Basic Accounting Theory. *A Statement of Basic Accounting Theory* [ASOBAT]. Evanston, Ill.: American Accounting Association, 1966.

American Accounting Association (1969). Committee on External Reporting. An Evaluation of External Reporting Practices — A Report of the 1966-68 Committee on External Reporting. *The Accounting Review* 44 (Supplement, 1969) 79-123.

American Accounting Association (1971a). Report of the Committee on Accounting Theory Construction and Verification. *The Accounting Review* 46 (Supplement, 1971) 53-79.

American Accounting Association (1971b). Report of the Committee on Behavioral Science Content of the Accounting Curriculum. *The Accounting Review* 46 (Supplement, 1971) 247-85.

American Accounting Association (1972). Report of the Committee on Research Methodology in Accounting. *The Accounting Review* 47 (Supplement, 1972) 399-520.

American Accounting Association (1974). Report of the Committee on Concepts and Standards — Internal Planning and Control. *The Accounting Review* 49 (Supplement, 1974) 79-96.

American Institute of (Certified Public) Accountants (1953). Committee on Terminology. "Review and Resume." *Accounting Terminology Bulletin No. 1* New York: American Institute of (Certified Public) Accountants, 1953.

American Institute of Certified Public Accountants (1970). Accounting Principles Board. *Basic Concepts and Accounting Principles Underlying Financial Statements of Business Enterprises.* Statement No. 4 of the Accounting Principles Board, 1970.

American Institute of Certified Public Accountants (1971). Accounting Principles Board. "Interest on Receivables and Payables." *APB Opinion No. 21.* New York: American Institute of Certified Public Accountants, 1971.

American Institute of Certified Public Accountants (1973). Study Group on the Objectives of Financial Statements. *Objectives of Financial Statements.* New York: American Institute of Certified Public Accountants, 1973.

Archibald, T. R. (1972). "Stock Market Reaction to the Depreciation Switch-Back." *The Accounting Review* 47 (January, 1972) 22-30.

Arrow, K. J. (1962). "Economic Welfare and the Allocation of Resources for Invention." In *The Rate and Direction of Economic Activity: Economic and Social Factors.* Princeton, N.J.: National Bureau of Economic Research. Princeton University Press, 1962.

Arrow, K. J. (1963). *Social Choice and Individual Values.* Revised Edition. New York: Yale University Press, 1963.

Arrow, K. J. (1964). "The Role of Securities in the Optimal Allocation of Risk-Bearing." *Review of Economic Studies* 31 (April, 1964) 91-6.

Arrow, K. J., and F. H. Hahn (1971). *General Competitive Analysis.* San Francisco: Holden-Day, Inc., 1971.

Baiman, S. (1975). "The Evaluation and Choice of Internal Information Systems Within a Multiperson World." *Journal of Accounting Research* 13 (Spring, 1975) 1-15.

Baker, H. K., and J. A. Haslen (1973). "Information Needs of Individual Investors." *The Journal of Accountancy* 136 (November, 1973) 64-9.

Ball, R. J. (1972). "Changes in Accounting Techniques and Stock Prices." *Journal of Accounting Research* 10 (Supplement, 1972) 1-40.

Ball, R. J., and P. Brown (1968). "An Empirical Evaluation of Accounting Income Numbers." *Journal of Accounting Research* 6 (Autumn, 1968) 159-77.

Ball, R. J., B. Lev, and R. Watts (1976). "Income Variation and Balance Sheet Compositions." *Journal of Accounting Research* 14 (Spring, 1976) 1-9.

Ball, R. J., and R. Watts (1972). "Some Time Series Properties of Accounting Income." *The Journal of Finance* 27 (June, 1972) 663-81.

Baskin, E. F. (1972). "The Communicative Effectiveness of Consistency Exceptions." *The Accounting Review* 47 (January, 1972) 38-51.

Beaver, W. H. (1968). "The Information Content of Annual Earnings Announcements." *Journal of Accounting Research* 6 (Supplement, 1968) 67-92.

Beaver, W. H. (1970). "The Time Series Behavior of Earnings." *Journal of Accounting Research* 8 (Supplement, 1970) 62-99.

Beaver, W. H. (1972). "The Behavior of Security Prices and Its Implications for Accounting Research (Methods)." Chapter II. Report of the Committee on Research Methodology in Accounting [AAA, 1972]. *The Accounting Review* 47 (Supplement, 1972) 407-37.

Beaver, W. H., and J. S. Demski (1974). "The Nature of Financial Accounting Objectives: A Summary and Synthesis." *Journal of Accounting Research* 12 (Supplement, 1974) 170-187.

Beaver, W. H., and R. E. Dukes (1972). "Interperiod Tax Allocation, Earnings Expectations, and the Behavior of Security Prices." *The Accounting Review* 47 (April, 1972) 320-32.

Beaver, W. H., and R. E. Dukes (1973). "Interperiod Tax Allocation and δ-Depreciation Methods: Some Empirical Results." *The Accounting Review* 45 (July, 1973) 549-59.

Beaver, W. H., J. W. Kennelly, and W. M. Voss (1968). "Predictive Ability as a Criterion for the Evaluation of Accounting Data." *The Accounting Review* 43 (October, 1968) 675-83.

Beaver, W. H., P. Kettler, and M. Scholes (1970). "The Association Between Market Determined and Accounting Determined Risk Measures." *The Accounting Review* 45 (October, 1970) 654-82.

Benston, G. J. (1973). "Required Disclosure and the Stock Market: An Evaluation of the Securities Exchange Act of 1934." *The American Economic Review* 63 (March, 1973) 132-55.

Bibliography

Bildersee, J. S. (1975). "The Association Between a Market-Determined Measure of Risk and Alternative Measures of Risk." *The Accounting Review* 50 (January, 1975) 81-98.

Birnberg, J. G., and R. Nath (1967). "Implications of Behavioral Science for Managerial Accounting." *The Accounting Review* 42 (July, 1967) 468-79.

Blaug, M. (1976). "Kuhn versus Lakatos, or Paradigms versus Research Programmes in the History of Economics." *History of Political Economy* 8 (January, 1976) 399-433.

Boatsman, J. R., and J. C. Robertson (1974). "Policy-Capturing on Selected Materiality Judgments." *The Accounting Review* 49 (April, 1974) 342-52.

Bradish, R. D. (1965). "Corporate Reporting and the Financial Analyst." *The Accounting Review* 40 (October, 1965) 757-66.

Brenner, V., and R. Shuey (1972). "An Empirical Study of Support for APB Opinion No. 16." *Journal of Accounting Research* 10 (Spring, 1972) 200-8.

Brown, P., and R. Ball (1967). "Some Preliminary Findings on the Association Between the Earnings of a Firm, Its Industry and the Economy." *Journal of Accounting Research* 5 (Supplement, 1967) 55-77.

Butterfield, H. (1957). *The Origins of Modern Science 1300-1800*. Revised Edition. New York: The Free Press, 1957.

Buzby, S. L. (1974). "Selected Items of Information and Their Disclosure in Annual Reports." *The Accounting Review* 49 (July, 1974) 423-35.

Canning, J. B. (1929). *The Economics of Accountancy*. New York: The Ronald Press Company, 1929.

Carsberg, B., J. Arnold and A. Hope (1977). "Predictive Value: A Criterion for Choice of Accounting Method" in W. T. Baxter and Sidney Davidson, eds. *Studies in Accounting Theory*. 3rd Edition. Homewood, Ill.: Richard D. Irwin, Inc., 1977 (forthcoming).

Cerf, A. R. (1961). *Corporate Reporting and Investment Decisions*. Berkeley: University of California Press, 1961.

Chambers, R. J. (1955). "Blueprint for a Theory of Accounting." *Accounting Research* 6 (January, 1955) 17-25.

Chambers, R. J. (1965). "The Development of Accounting Theory" in R. J. Chambers, L. Goldberg, and R. L. Mathews, eds. *The Accounting Frontier*. Melbourne: Cheshire, 1965, pp. 18-35.

Chambers, R. J. (1966). *Accounting, Evaluation and Economic Behavior*. Englewood Cliffs: Prentice-Hall, Inc., 1966.

Chandra, G. (1974). "A Study of the Consensus on Disclosure Among Public Accountants and Security Analysts." *The Accounting Review* 49 (October, 1974) 733-42.

Clark, J. M. (1923). *Studies in the Economics of Overhead Costs*. Chicago, Ill.: University of Chicago Press, 1923.

Copeland, R. M., A. J. Francia, and R. H. Strawser (1973). "Students as Subjects in Behavioral Business Research." *The Accounting Review* 48 (April, 1973) 365-74.

Debreu, G. (1959). *Theory of Value*. Cowles Foundation Monograph 17. New York: John Wiley & Sons, Inc., 1959.

Demsetz, H. (1969). "Information and Efficiency: Another Viewpoint." *The Journal of Law and Economics* 12 (April, 1969) 1-22.

Demski, J. S. (1972). *Information Analysis*. Reading, Mass.: Addison-Wesley Publishing Co., 1972.

Demski, J. S. (1973a). "The General Impossibility of Normative Accounting Standards." *The Accounting Review* 48 (October, 1973) 718-23.

Demski, J. S. (1973b). "Rational Choice of Accounting Method for a Class of Partnerships." *Journal of Accounting Research* 11 (Autumn, 1973) 176-90.

Demski, J. S., and G. A. Feltham (1976). *Cost Determination: A Conceptual Approach*. Ames, Iowa: The Iowa State University Press, 1976.

Dermer, J. D. (1973). "Cognitive Characteristics and the Perceived Importance of Information." *The Accounting Review* 48 (July, 1973) 511-19.

Devine, C. T. (1960). "Research Methodology and Accounting Theory Formation." *The Accounting Review* 35 (July, 1960) 387-99.

✓ Dickhaut, J. W., and I. R. C. Eggleton (1975). "An Examination of the Processes Underlying Comparative Judgements of Numerical Stimuli." *Journal of Accounting Research* 13 (Spring, 1975) 38-72.

✓ Driver, M. J., and T. J. Mock (1975). "Human Information Processing, Decision Style Theory, and Accounting Information Systems." *The Accounting Review* 50 (July, 1975) 490-508.

Driver, M. J., and S. Streufert (1969). "Integrative Complexity: An Approach to Individuals and Groups as Information-Processing Systems." *Administrative Science Quarterly* 14 (June, 1969) 272-85.

Due, J. F., and A. F. Friedlaender (1973). *Government Finance: Economics of the Public Sector.* Homewood, Ill.: Richard D. Irwin, Inc., 1973.

✓ Dyckman, T. R., M. Gibbins, and R. J. Swieringa (1975). "Experimental and Survey Research in Financial Accounting: A Review and Evaluation." *The Impact of Accounting Research in Financial Accounting and Disclosure on Accounting Practice.* Durham, N. C.: Duke University, Unpublished Proceedings, 1975.

Dyer, J. (1973). "A Search for Objective Materiality Norms in Accounting and Auditing." Unpublished D.B.A. Dissertation. University of Kentucky, 1973.

Ecton, W. W. (1969). "Communication Through Accounting — Bankers' Views." *The Journal of Accountancy* 128 (August, 1969) 79-81.

Edwards, E. O., and P. W. Bell (1961). *The Theory and Measurement of Business Income.* Berkeley, Calif.: University of California Press, 1961.

Falk, H., and T. Ophir (1973a). "The Effect of Risk on the Use of Financial Statements by Investment Decision-Makers: A Case Study." *The Accounting Review* 48 (April, 1973) 323-38.

✓ Falk, H., and T. Ophir (1973b). "The Influence of Differences in Accounting Policies on Investment Decisions." *Journal of Accounting Research* 11 (Spring, 1973) 108-16.

✓ Fama, E. F. (1970). "Efficient Capital Markets: A Review of Theory and Empirical Work." *The Journal of Finance* 25 (May, 1970) 383-417.

✓ Fama, E. F., L. Fisher, M. C. Jensen, and R. Roll (1969). "The Adjustment of Stock Prices to New Information." *International Economic Review* 10 (February, 1969) 1-21.

Fama, E. F., and A. B. Laffer (1971). "Information and Capital Markets." *The Journal of Business* 44 (July, 1971) 289-98.

✓ Feltham, G. A. (1972). *Information Evaluation.* Studies in Accounting Research #5. American Accounting Association, 1972.

Fetter, F. A. (1927). "Interest Theory and Price Movements." *The American Economic Review* 17 (Supplement, 1927) 62-105.

Fisher, I. (1906). *The Nature of Capital and Income.* New York: The Macmillan Company, 1906.

Fisher, I. (1927). *The Income Concept in the Light of Experience.* New Haven: Yale University Press, 1927.

Fisher, I. (1927). "Interest Theory and Price Movements — Discussion." *The American Economic Review* 17 (Supplement, 1927) 106-8.

✓ Friedman, M. (1953). "The Methodology of Positive Economics." *Essays in Positive Economics.* Chicago: University of Chicago Press, 1953.

Gilman, S. (1939). *Accounting Concepts of Profit.* New York: The Ronald Press Company, 1939.

Godwin, L. B. (1975). "CPA and User Opinions on Increased Corporate Disclosure." *The CPA Journal* 45 (July, 1975) 31-5.

✓ Gonedes, N. J. (1972). "Efficient Capital Markets and External Accounting." *The Accounting Review* 47 (January, 1972) 11-21.

Gonedes, N. J. (1973). "Evidence on the Information Content of Accounting Numbers:

Bibliography

Accounting-Based and Market-Based Estimates of Systematic Risk." *Journal of Financial and Quantitative Analysis* 8 (June, 1973) 407-43.

Gonedes, N. J. (1974). "Capital Market Equilibrium and Annual Accounting Numbers: Empirical Evidence." *Journal of Accounting Research* 12 (Spring, 1974) 26-62.

Gonedes, N. J. (1975). "Information Production and Capital Market Equilibrium." *The Journal of Finance* 30 (June, 1975) 841-64.

Gonedes, N. J., and N. Dopuch (1974). "Capital Market Equilibrium, Information Production, and Selecting Accounting Techniques: Theoretical Framework and Review of Empirical Work." *Journal of Accounting Research* 12 (Supplement, 1974) 48-129.

Gonedes, N. J., N. Dopuch, and S. Penman (1975). "Disclosure Rules, Information Production and Capital Market Equilibrium: The Case of Disclosure Rules." Unpublished Working Paper, Graduate School of Business, University of Chicago, June, 1975.

Grady, P. (1965). *An Inventory of Generally Accepted Accounting Principles for Business Enterprises.* Accounting Research Study No. 7. New York: American Institute of Certified Public Accountants, 1965.

Grossman, S. J., and J. E. Stiglitz (1976). "Information and Competitive Price Systems." *The American Economic Review* 66 (May, 1976) 246-53.

Haley, C. W., and L. D. Schall (1973). *The Theory of Financial Decisions.* New York: McGraw-Hill Book Company, 1973.

Haried, A. A. (1972). "The Semantic Dimensions of Financial Statements." *Journal of Accounting Research* 10 (Autumn, 1972) 376-91.

Haried, A. A. (1973). "Measurement of Meaning in Financial Reports." *Journal of Accounting Research* 11 (Spring, 1973) 117-45.

Hart, O.D. (1975). "On the Optimality of Equilibrium When Markets are Incomplete." *Journal of Economic Theory* 11 (December, 1975) 418-43.

Hatfield, H. R. (1927). *Accounting.* New York: D. Appleton & Company, 1927.

Hayami, Y., and W. Peterson (1972). "Social Returns to Public Information Services: Statistical Reporting of U.S. Farm Commodities." *The American Economic Review* 62 (March, 1972) 119-30.

Henderson, J. M., and R. E. Quandt (1971). *Microeconomic Theory: A Mathematical Approach,* 2nd ed. New York: McGraw-Hill Book Company, 1971.

Hicks, J. R. (1939). *Value and Capital.* London: Oxford University Press, 1939.

Hirshleifer, J. (1971). "The Private and Social Value of Information and the Reward to Inventive Activity." *The American Economic Review* 61 (September, 1971) 561-74.

Hirshleifer, J. (1973). "Where Are We in the Theory of Information?" *The American Economic Review* 63 (May, 1973) 31-9.

Ho, Y. C., and K. C. Chu (1974). "Information Structure in Dynamic Multi-Person Control Problems." *Automatica* 10 (1974) 341-51.

Hofstedt, T. R. (1972). "Some Behavioral Parameters of Financial Analysis." *The Accounting Review* 47 (October, 1972) 679-92.

Hofstedt, T. R. (1976). "Behavioral Accounting Research: Pathologies, Paradigms and Prescriptions." *Accounting, Organizations and Society* 1 (Spring, 1976) 43-58.

Horngren, C. T. (1955). "Security Analysts and the Price Level." *The Accounting Review* 30 (October, 1955) 575-81.

Horngren, C. T. (1956). "The Funds Statement and Its Use by Analysts." *The Journal of Accountancy* 101 (January, 1956) 55-9.

Horngren, C. T. (1957). "Depreciation, Flow of Funds and the Price Level." *Financial Analysts Journal* 13 (August, 1957) 45-7.

Ijiri, Y. (1975). *Theory of Accounting Measurement.* Studies in Accounting Research #10. American Accounting Association, 1975.

Ijiri, Y., and R. K. Jaedicke (1966). "Reliability and Objectivity of Accounting Measurements." *The Accounting Review* 41 (July, 1966) 474-83.

Jaffe, J. F. (1974). "Special Information and Insider Trading." *The Journal of Business* 47 —July, 1974) 410-28.

Kaplan, R. S. (1975). "The Information Content of Financial Accounting Numbers: A Survey of Empirical Evidence." *The Impact of Accounting Research in Financial Accounting and Disclosure on Accounting Practice.* Durham, N.C.: Duke University, Unpublished Proceedings, 1975.

Kaplan, R. S., and R. Roll (1972). "Investor Evaluation of Accounting Information: Some Empirical Evidence." *The Journal of Business* 45 (April, 1972) 225-57.

Kenley, W. J., and G. J. Staubus (1972). *Objectives and Concepts of Financial Statements.* Accounting Research Study No. 3. Accountancy Research Foundation (Australia), 1972, pp. 52-8.

Kihlstrom, R., and L. J. Mirman (1975). "Information and Market Equilibrium." *The Bell Journal of Economics* 6 (Spring, 1975) 357-76.

Kihlstrom, R., and M. Pauly (1971). "The Role of Insurance in the Allocation of Risk." *The American Economic Review* 61 (May, 1971) 371-9.

King, B. (1966). "Market and Industry Factors in Stock Price Behavior." *The Journal of Business* 39 (January, 1966) 139-90.

Knight, F. (1933). *The Economic Organization.* Chicago: The University of Chicago Press, 1933.

Kuhn, T. S. (1970). *The Structure of Scientific Revolutions.* 2nd Edition, Enlarged. Chicago: The University of Chicago Press, 1970.

Lakatos, I., and A. Musgrave, eds. (1970). *Criticism and the Growth of Knowledge.* New York: Cambridge University Press, 1970.

Lev, B., and S. Kunitzky (1974). "On the Association Between Smoothing Measures and the Risk of Common Stocks." *The Accounting Review* 49 (April, 1974) 259-70.

Libby, R. (1975a). "The Use of Simulated Decision Makers in Information Evaluation." *The Accounting Review.* 50 (July, 1975) 475-89.

Libby, R. (1975b). "Accounting Ratios and the Prediction of Failure: Some Behavioral Evidence." *Journal of Accounting Research* 13 (Spring, 1975) 150-61.

Littleton, A. C. (1953). *Structure of Accounting Theory.* Monograph No. 5. American Accounting Association, 1953.

Luce, R. D., and H. Raiffa (1957). *Games and Decisions: Introduction and Critical Survey.* New York: John Wiley & Sons, Inc., 1957.

MacNeal, K. (1939). *Truth in Accounting.* Philadelphia: University of Pennsylvania Press, 1939.

Magee, R. P. (1974). "Industry-wide Commonalities in Earnings." *Journal of Accounting Research* 12 (Autumn, 1974) 270-87.

Malinvaud, E. (1972). *Lectures in Microeconomic Theory.* Amsterdam: North-Holland Publishing Company, 1972.

Marschak, J., and R. Radner (1972). *Economic Theory of Teams.* New Haven and London: Yale University Press, 1972.

Marshall, J. (1974). "Private Incentives and Public Information." *The American Economic Review* 64 (June, 1974) 373-90.

Marshall, R. M. (1975). "Interpreting the API." *The Accounting Review* 50 (January, 1975) 99-111.

May, G. O. (1943). *Financial Accounting.* New York: The Macmillan Co., 1943.

May, R. G. (1971). "The Influence of Quarterly Earnings Announcements on Investor Decisions as Reflected in Common Stock Price Changes." *Journal of Accounting Research* 9 (Supplement, 1971) 119-63.

May, R. G., and G. L. Sundem (1973). "Cost of Information and Security Prices: Market Association Tests for Accounting Policy Decisions." *The Accounting Review* 48 (January, 1973) 80-94.

McDonald, D. L. (1967). "Feasibility Criteria for Accounting Measures." *The Accounting Review* 42 (October, 1967) 662-79.

Bibliography

Miller, D., and L. A. Gordon (1975). "Conceptual Levels and the Design of Accounting Information Systems." *Decision Sciences* 6 (April, 1975) 259-69.

Moonitz, M. (1961). *The Basic Postulates of Accounting.* Accounting Research Study No. 1. New York: American Institute of Certified Public Accountants, 1961.

Nagel, E. (1963). "Assumptions in Economic Theory." *The American Economic Review* 53 (May, 1963) 211-9.

Nelson, K., and R. H. Strawser (1970). "A Note on APB Opinion No. 16." *Journal of Accounting Research* 8 (Autumn, 1970) 284-9.

Ng, D. (1975). "Information Accuracy and Social Welfare Under Honogeneous Beliefs." *Journal of Financial Economics* 2 (March, 1975) 53-70.

Paton, W. A. (1922). *Accounting Theory.* New York: The Ronald Press Company, 1922.

Paton, W. A., and A. C. Littleton (1940). *An Introduction to Corporate Accounting Standards.* Monograph No. 3. American Accounting Association, 1940.

Pattillo, J. W. (1975). "Materiality: the (Formerly) Elusive Standard." *Financial Executive* 43 (August, 1975) 20-7.

Pattillo, J. W., and J. D. Siebel (1973). "Quantitative Measures of Materiality." *Financial Executive* 41 (October, 1973) 31-2, 37-8.

Pattillo, J. W. (1975). "Materiality: the (Formerly) Elusive Standard." *Financial Executive* 43 (August, 1975) 20-7.

Quirk, J., and R. Saposnik (1968). *Introduction to General Equilibrium Theory and Welfare Economics.* New York: McGraw-Hill Book Company, 1968.

Radner, R. (1974). "Market Equilibrium and Uncertainty: Concepts and Problems" in *Frontiers of Quantitative Economics,* Vol. II. M. D. Intriligator and D. A. Kendrick, eds. Amsterdam: North-Holland Publishing Company, 1974.

Revsine, L. (1970a). "On the Correspondence Between Replacement Cost Income and Economic Income." *The Accounting Review* 45 (July, 1970) 513-23.

Revsine, L. (1970b). "Data Expansion and Conceptual Structure." *The Accounting Review* 45 (October, 1970) 704-11.

Revsine, L. (1970c). "Change in Budget Pressure and Its Impact on Supervisor Behavior." *Journal of Accounting Research* 8 (Autumn, 1970) 90-2.

Revsine, L. (1973). *Replacement Cost Accounting.* Englewood Cliffs, N. J.: Prentice-Hall, Inc., 1973.

Revsine, L. (1975). "Towards Greater Comparability in Accounting Reports." *Financial Analysts Journal* 31 (January-February, 1975) 45-51.

Rhode, J. G. (1972). "Behavioral Science Methodologies with Application for Accounting Research: References and Source Materials." Chapter VII. Report of the Committee on Research Methodology in Accounting [AAA, 1972]. *The Accounting Review* 47 (Supplement, 1972) 494-504.

Rose, J., W. Beaver, S. Becker and G. Sorter (1970). "Toward an Empirical Measure of Materiality." *Journal of Accounting Research* 8 (Supplement, 1970) 138-56.

Samuelson, P. A. (1963). "Problems of Methodology: Discussion." *The American Economic Review* 53 (May, 1963) 231-6.

Sanders, T. H., H. R. Hatfield, and U. Moore (1938). *A Statement of Accounting Principles.* New York: American Institute of (Certified Public) Accountants, 1938.

Savage, L. J. (1954). *The Foundations of Statistics.* New York: John Wiley & Sons, Inc., 1954.

Scitovsky, T. (1971). *Welfare and Competition.* Revised Edition. Homewood, Ill.: Richard D. Irwin, Inc., 1971.

Schroder, N. M., M. J. Driver and S. Streufert (1967). *Human Information Processing.* New York: Holt, Rinehart and Winston, Inc., 1967.

Securities and Exchange Commission (1976). "Notice of Adoption of Amendments to Regulation S-X Requiring Disclosure of Certain Replacement Cost Data." *Accounting Series Release No. 190* (March 23, 1976).

✓Sharpe, W. F. (1963). "A Simplified Model for Portfolio Analysis." *Management Science* 9 (1963) 277-93.

Singhvi, S. S., and H. B. Desai (1971). "An Empirical Analysis of the Quality of Corporate Financial Disclosure." *The Accounting Review* 46 (January, 1971) 129-38.

Smith, J. E., and N. P. Smith (1971). "Readability: A Measure of the Performance of the Communication Function of Financial Reporting." *The Accounting Review* 46 (July, 1971) 552-61.

Snavely, H. (1967). "Accounting Information Criteria." *The Accounting Review* 42 (April, 1967) 223-32.

Soper, F. J., and R. Dolphin, Jr. (1964). "Readability and Corporate Annual Reports." *The Accounting Review* 39 (April, 1964) 358-62.

✓Sorter, G. H. (1969). "An 'Events' Approach to Basic Accounting Theory." *The Accounting Review* 44 (January, 1969) 12-19.

Spence, M. (1973). "Job Market Signaling." *The Quarterly Journal of Economics* 87 (August, 1973) 355-74.

✓Spence, M., and R. Zeckhauser (1971). "Insurance, Information, and Individual Action." *The American Economic Review* 61 (May, 1971) 380-7.

Sprouse, R. T., and M. Moonitz (1962). *A Tentative Set of Broad Accounting Principles for Business Enterprises.* Accounting Research Study No. 3. New York: American Institute of Certified Public Accountants, 1962.

Staubus, G. J. (1954). "An Accounting Concept of Revenue." Unpublished Ph.D. dissertation, Graduate School of Business, University of Chicago, 1954.

Staubus, G. J. (1961). *A Theory of Accounting to Investors.* Berkeley, Calif.: University of California Press, 1961.

Staubus, G. J. (1967). "Current Cash Equivalents for Assets: A Dissent." *The Accounting Review* 42 (October, 1967) 650-61.

Staubus, G. J. (1970). "Determinants of the Value of Accounting Procedures." *Abacus* (December, 1970) 105-19.

Staubus, G. J. (1971). "The Relevance of Evidence on Cash Flows." In *Asset Valuation and Income Determination.* R. R. Sterling, ed. Lawrence, Kan.: Scholars Book Company, 1971, pp. 42-69.

Staubus, G. J. (1976). "The Multiple-Criteria Approach to Making Accounting Decisions." *Accounting and Business Research* 6 (Autumn, 1976) 276-88.

◦ Sterling, R. (1967). "A Statement of Basic Accounting Theory: A Review Article." *Journal of Accounting Research* 5 (Spring, 1967) 95-112.

Sterling, R., (1970a). *Theory of the Measurement of Enterprise Income.* Lawrence, Kan.: University Press of Kansas, 1970.

Sterling, R. (1970b). "On Theory Construction and Verification." *The Accounting Review* 45 (July, 1970) 444-57.

Sterling, R. (1972a). "Introduction." *Research Methodology in Accounting.* R. Sterling, ed., Lawrence, Kan.; Scholars Book Co., 1972, pp. 1-7. [Note: papers which appear in A.A.A. (1972), cited above — including Beaver (1972), and Rhode (1972) — appear in this volume as well, together with discussions.]

Sterling, R. (1972b). "Decision Oriented Financial Accounting." *Accounting and Business Research* 2 (Summer, 1972) 198-208.

✓ Sterling, R., and W. Harrison (1974). "Discussion of Capital Market Equilibrium, Information Production, and Selecting Accounting Techniques: Theoretical Framework and Review of Empirical Work." *Journal of Accounting Research* 12 (Supplement, 1974) 142-57.

✓ Stiglitz, J. E. (1975). "Incentive, Risk and Information: Notes Toward a Theory of Hierarchy." *The Bell Journal of Economics* 6 (Autumn, 1975) 552-79.

Streufert, S. (1970). "Complexity and Complex Decision Making: Convergences Between Differentiation and Integration Approaches to the Prediction of Task Performance." *Journal of Experimental Social Psychology* 6 (October, 1970) 494-509.

Bibliography

Streufert, S., and Schroder, H. M. (1965). "Conceptual Structure, Environmental Complexity and Task Performance." *Journal of Experimental Research in Personality* 1 (October, 1965) 132-7.

Sunder, S. (1973). "Relations Between Accounting Changes and Stock Prices: Problems of Measurement and Some Empirical Evidence." *Journal of Accounting Research* 11 (Supplement, 1973) 1-45.

Sweeney, H. W. (1930). "Maintenance of Capital." *The Accounting Review* 5 (December, 1930) 277-87.

Sweeney, H. W. (1932). "Stabilized Appreciation." *The Accounting Review* 7 (June, 1932) 115-21.

Sweeney, H. W. (1933a). "Capital." *The Accounting Review* 8 (September, 1933) 185-99.

Sweeney, H. W. (1933b). "Income." *The Accounting Review* 8 (December, 1933) 323-35.

Sweeney, H. W. (1936). *Stabilized Accounting*. New York: Harper & Brothers, 1936.

Thomas, A. L. (1969). *The Allocation Problem in Financial Accounting*. Studies in Accounting Research #3. American Accounting Association, 1969.

Thomas, A. L. (1974). *The Allocation Problem: Part Two*. Studies in Accounting Research #9. American Accounting Association, 1974.

Vatter, W. J. (1947). *The Fund Theory of Accounting and Its Implications for Financial Reports*. Studies in Business Administration XVII, 2. Chicago: The University of Chicago Press, 1947.

von Neumann, J., and O. Morgenstern (1947). *Theory of Games and Economic Behavior*. Princeton, N. J.: Princeton University Press, 1947.

Wells, M. C. (1976). "A Revolution in Accounting Thought?" *The Accounting Review* 51 (July, 1976) 471-82.

Wilcox, E. B. (1941). "Comments on 'An Introduction to Corporate Accounting Standards.'" *The Accounting Review* 16 (March, 1941) 75-81.

Wilson, R. (1974). "Information in an Equilibrium Model." *Working Paper No. 42*. Institute for Mathematical Studies in the Social Sciences, Stanford University, 1974.

Woolsey, S. M. (1973). "Materiality Survey." *The Journal of Accountancy* 136 (September, 1973) 91-2.